I Ching

WALKING YOUR PATH, CREATING YOUR FUTURE

HILARY BARRETT

ARCTURUS

ACKNOWLEDGEMENTS

I owe a great debt and heartfelt thanks to many people, especially:

My husband David for the gift of his time, skill and care in improving the text.

Lise Heyboer for sharing her beautiful, honest *Yijing* at http://yijing.nl and kindly allowing me to use her images of the Chinese characters.

Bradford Hatcher for sharing his profound and scholarly work at http://hermetica.info and for valuable suggestions on the text.

And also to S.J. Marshall, whose *Mandate of Heaven* transformed my understanding of many hexagrams (especially Hexagram 55), and Stephen Karcher, author of *Total I Ching*, for formative guidance and insight.

And thank you to all the people I've had the honour of reading for over the years, and all the members of my site's *I Ching Community*, for sharing your experiences, wisdom and understanding.

ARCTURUS

This edition published in 2011 by Arcturus Publishing Limited
26/27 Bickels Yard, 151–153 Bermondsey Street,
London SE1 3HA

Design and layout copyright © 2010 Arcturus Publishing Limited
Text copyright © 2010 Hilary Barrett

ISBN: 978-1-84837-453-9
AD001153EN

Printed in Singapore

Contents

Introduction: *What is the I Ching?*

An oracle

The I Ching is an oracle: something that speaks. Although it comes disguised as a book, it is really a voice in a conversation, and you can talk with it (or with what speaks through it) as you would with a wise friend and mentor.

Talking with an oracle is called divination. When you divine, you listen attentively to hear the question you are asking, and the oracle's answer, and your own response of recognition. In a world that seems noisier than ever, divination offers a quiet refuge for listening. It is the place where your inner guidance comes into resonance with present truth, so that it can never be swallowed up in the circumstantial clamour of reasons, emotions and opinions.

The I Ching is an oracle; it is not a slot machine to dispense ready-made answers. It will not tell you what to do, or deny your free will by predicting a future set in stone. It gives you insight into the present moment – and who is to say how much of the future is contained within that? It will take you under the surface of experience, into its inner currents, where you can participate in their flow.

The Change Book

 'I Ching' – or Yijing, in the more modern way of transliterating the Chinese – means 'Change Book' or 'Classic of Changes'. 'Ching' (Jing) is a title given to books of especial importance, while 'I' (Yi), the name of the oracle, simply means 'Change'. The earliest way of writing 'Yi' probably shows the sun emerging from behind the clouds: change that comes as a gift.

The Yijing is a complete guide to change: understanding it, moving with it, creating it. It describes change that is transformative and seasonal, global and personal, incremental and revolutionary. It tells stories of great historical change, and it sketches tiny vignettes of everyday life – marrying, surviving an illness, repairing a well.

Origins

The Yijing has its roots in unknowably old spoken traditions, but its earliest texts were first written down about 3000 years ago in China by the Zhou people: these texts are known as the Zhouyi, the Zhou Changes. The Yi has grown from these ancient roots and has been in continuous use ever since, in unbroken conversation with generations of diviners through the millennia.

Those who consulted with the oracle added their own thoughts to it – practical, spiritual and philosophical – and by around 200 CE the most perceptive of the early commentaries had been compiled into the Yi's Ten Wings. The original oracle and line texts (the Zhouyi) together with the Ten Wings make up the Yijing.

Elements

LINES AND CHANGES

The Yijing combines words with a basic structure of lines – as you can see in the main part of this book, where each hexagram is identified both by its six lines, and by its name. The structure lends order to the words, creates meaning and relationships of its own, and provides the way of consulting the Yijing by casting a hexagram.

The original building blocks of the hexagrams could not be simpler. There are just two: a solid line, and a broken line:

The solid, closed line is firm and strong; the broken, open line is flexible and soft. They represent the basic concepts of yang and yin: the two fundamental, complementary forces and qualities in the universe that sustain and give rise to one another.

Yang, the solid line, is dynamic; it begins things and drives them forward. Yin, the broken line, is more passive and responsive, receiving the yang impulse and growing it into something real.

In the constant, universal cycle of change, beings with yin qualities are always becoming more yang, while yang becomes more yin. We see this in natural cycles of change: the sun shines out (yang), then sets (yin); the moon wanes (yin) and waxes (yang); the summer changes to autumn and winter changes to spring.

Exactly the same change takes place within the Yijing, where the solid and broken lines are always changing into one another. A 'young' line is stable and does not yet show signs of change; an 'old' line is in the process of changing. This creates four kinds of line. The basic solid and broken lines represent the 'young' states of yin and yang, and then each is marked to show when it is 'old', like this:

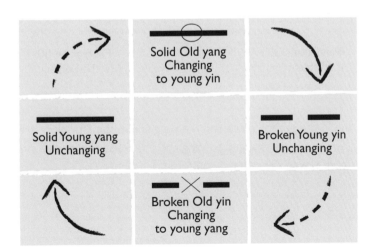

In theory, the young lines are in the process of becoming old, but they don't actually change in the course of a reading.

from lines to hexagrams

A hexagram is a stack of six lines, built from the bottom up, like a house – or you could say it grows from the ground up, like a tree. In each of the Yijing's sixty-four hexagrams, the pattern of broken and solid lines represents a unique interaction of yin and yang.

To begin a conversation with Yi, you ask a question and cast a single hexagram to receive its answer (see 'Casting a hexagram', page 12). This first hexagram, which captures the essence of what is involved, is identified just by its pattern of the two basic kinds of line, solid (yang) or broken (yin).

In addition, each line as you cast it may be young, and stable, or old, and changing to its opposite. If there are no changing lines, the single hexagram you cast is your whole answer. If you have changing lines, you let them change and then draw a *second* hexagram, in which the young lines you cast stay the same, and the old lines have changed – old yang becoming yin, old yin becoming yang. In this way, all of the sixty-four hexagrams can change into one another.

For example:

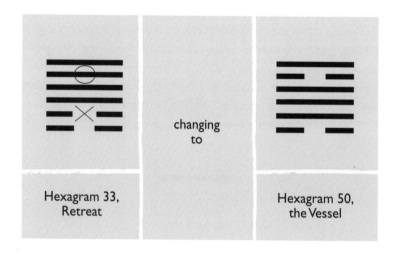

Hexagram 33, Retreat

changing to

Hexagram 50, the Vessel

In this reading, the yin line in the second place and the yang line in the fifth place are old, changing lines. So in the second hexagram, line 2 has changed to yang and line 5 has changed to yin, while the other, young, unchanging lines have stayed the same.

The eight trigrams

Hexagrams are made of six lines, trigrams of three, so that each hexagram can be read as the meeting of two trigrams. The hexagrams represent often quite complex situations; the trigrams are simpler and more elemental.

Understanding the trigrams in your readings gives you insight into the hexagram as a landscape of their energies, with the relationship of lower and upper trigrams suggesting a relationship between your inner and outer worlds. Trigrams are also the key to the Image section, which describes how a wise person would work with their energies to meet the challenges of each hexagram.

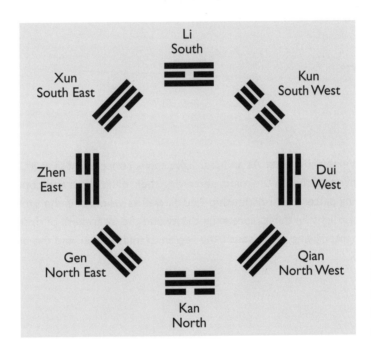

The 'King Wen' arrangement of the eight trigrams. (The bottom line of each trigram is nearest to the centre.)

ZHEN, THUNDER

Thunder is shock, upheaval and the spark of the new. In old Chinese belief, thunder slept in the earth over winter and erupted from it in spring, awakening living things into new growth. Thunder is our basic drive for renewal; he inspires initiative and decisive action; he is the stimulus that sets things in motion.

He is the eldest son in the trigram family: the first connection of heaven (potential) with earth (realization). Yang makes itself known here, emerging into the field and beginning to grow. Thunder belongs to the east and to spring.

XUN, WIND OR WOOD

Xun is both wind and living plants: whatever penetrates, spreads and grows, shaping itself to the space available, or shaping that space to its own nature. She is responsive flexibility, sensitively improvising and adapting. Like the wind, she can always find a way through because she never creates any resistance, and so her influence is subtle and gradual but far-reaching.

In the family of trigrams, Xun is the eldest daughter, gentle and submissive. She belongs to the southeast, and to late spring and early summer.

LI, FIRE AND LIGHT

Li is fire and light, both inner and outer. As an inner light, she is consciousness at its most lucid and unclouded, holding things together in the mind, perceiving their differences and connections and discerning the underlying patterns of relationship. And as well as vision, Li is the light that makes things visible: the power to cast light on things, spreading clarity and the awareness of order.

Li is the middle daughter, living in the south, the region of midsummer and the burning sun.

KUN, EARTH

Kun is earth: open to receive and support what comes to her, providing for its full development. She makes inspiration manifest, gives it form and sustains its growth. Earth is available to be used, ready to lend her strength to the work without limit. She protects and accepts all things in their totality – present and potential – in an unconditional embrace.

Earth is mother, found in the southwest and the harvest time of late summer and early autumn.

DUI, LAKE OR MARSH

Dui is lake and marsh, abundant energy that teems with life. She is the impulse to communicate, share and exchange, and delights in both inner and outer conversation. She brings things into circulation and gives them voice. This is the sheer enjoyment of participating in life to the full, expressing ourselves and hearing others, and satisfying our desires.

Lake is the youngest daughter, spirit of the fertile west and of autumn.

QIAN, HEAVEN

Qian is suprahuman, cosmic law. Enduring, he determines the nature and development of all things, from the movement of the stars, to the cycle of the seasons, to causing each individual seed to grow into its own kind of plant.

Heaven is creativity in its pure form: the force that drives change, and what endures within it. He confronts us with truth and what it demands, both as the absolute law of nature, and as the challenge of individual calling, experienced as an inner law. He is both the awareness of what to do and how to be, and also the power to act on it.

Heaven is father, found in the northwest, the realm between autumn and winter, when the buds set and seeds fall to earth.

KAN, WATER

Kan is deep water, flowing and formless. He is the complement of Li – dark where Li is bright, unconscious to her sharp lucidity – and represents a more fluid, intuitive and emotional way of perceiving. This is danger, exposure and solitude, and the need to respond with courageous self-reliance when confronted by the haunting unknown.

Water is the middle son, situated in the north, associated with midwinter and midnight.

GEN, MOUNTAIN

The mountain is still; it is a limit where you must stop. Gen brings each cycle to an end, defining a space where we can recognize, assimilate and complete our experience. He creates a personal still centre amid change, where we can retreat for perspective, and a firm foundation for new growth. He is well grounded, confident and of independent spirit; he is still, and knows.

Mountain is the youngest son, child of maturity. In the cycle of directions and seasons, he is the northeast, late winter approaching spring, the pivot between cycles.

Talking with Change

A Yijing reading moves through three interlocking phases:

- *Opening* the channel
- *Connecting* to the response
- *Integrating* the answer

Everything you do to invite and receive a response from the oracle is part of opening the channel. Choosing and asking your question, casting your hexagram and tracing its changes – these are all part of creating a clear flow of communication. Then you connect to Yi's response: you relate to it personally, and find yourself in the reading's landscape. Finally, you integrate the reading into your life, translating it into practice and giving it an enduring place as part of your way of thinking and being.

OPENING

THE QUESTION

Your chosen question starts your conversation with the oracle, and it defines what you will hear in the response. Not that it limits what Yi can say – far from it – but it affects what you are listening for.

The help you can receive from a reading depends strongly on your question. The clearer you are about what you're asking, the easier you'll find it to understand and connect with the response. And the more conscious and intentional your question – the more clearly you know *why* you're asking – the easier it is to integrate and use the answer.

Before you phrase the question, immerse yourself in it: allow yourself time to recognize all the issues, hopes and fears involved. Form an intention for the reading: what would you like to change? (For instance, a decision made, movement closer to a goal, being more at peace with a situation.) Then ask as directly as possible for the help you need.

There are no rules about what to ask, but some questions work better than others, making it easier for you to interpret the response.

There are three basic questions you could ask, which cover almost everything:
- 'What's happening?'
- 'What can I do?' (Or, 'How can I respond creatively?')
- 'What if I tried doing this?' (Or, 'What if I continue on the same as before?')

That is, you might ask for insight, advice, or a prediction. And there is a fourth question:
- 'What do I need to be aware of now?'

This is a quieter, more meditative approach, simply opening yourself to whatever the universe has to tell you in this moment.

There are also two kinds of question that are best avoided, as they make for tremendously confusing answers:
- Asking for a 'yes' or 'no' response. (The Yijing has no hexagram or line for 'yes' or 'no'.)
- Asking about two alternatives in one question. (How would you know which alternative the answer is talking about?)

So instead of asking 'Will this happen?' ask 'What can I expect?' and instead of asking 'Should I do this?' ask 'What if I do this?' Then you are the one to decide what you should do.

There's no area of life you can't consult with Yi about, and no question is too huge ('What's my purpose in life?') or too trivial ('What if I wear the red suit to the interview?'). Here are a few example questions, just to give you an idea of the possibilities:
- 'What kind of relationship am I creating?'
- 'What should I hold in mind for this coming year?'
- 'How will I know when it is time to change my job?'
- 'What do I have to contribute to this project?'
- 'What am I in this situation to learn?'
- 'What changes should I expect at work?'
- 'How can we build a positive relationship?'
- 'What if I try encouraging him to talk?'
- 'What would it be like to live in this new house?'
- 'What is the message of this dream?'

CASTING A HEXAGRAM

Once you've written down your question, it's time to cast the hexagram. You will need three identical coins. To cast the first line, throw the three coins together. Each head counts three; each tail counts two. Add up the result – it will be 6, 7, 8 or 9. These numbers are a convenient way to refer to the four kinds of line:

COINS	TOTAL	LINE	
3 tails	6	changing broken line – old yin	▬ ✕ ▬
2 tails, 1 head	7	unchanging solid line – young	▬▬▬▬
2 heads, 1 tail	8	uchanging broken line – young yin	▬▬ ▬▬
3 heads,	9	changing solid line – old yang	▬▬◯▬▬

Write down the line you have received. This is the first line of your hexagram – the bottom line.

Repeat the same process five more times, working from the bottom up to the sixth and last line. These six lines are your cast hexagram – the *primary hexagram*, and key to your answer. You can look it up in the reference chart on page 16.

If all six lines are young (unchanging), this hexagram is your complete reading. The answer to your question comes from its Oracle, Image, Pair and Sequence.

If you cast one or more changing lines, then as well as reading those texts for the whole hexagram, you also read the ones for the changing lines you received.

Then, you let the changing lines change…

Every old yin   ▬✕▬   becomes young yang   ▬▬▬▬

Every old yang   ▬◯▬   becomes young yin   ▬▬ ▬▬

The other, young lines stay the same. This gives you your *relating hexagram*: you read only its Oracle, Image, Sequence and Pair.

CONNECTING

The next step is to connect with your reading. Be patient: allow time for the words and images to sink in, and for recognition to emerge. You don't have to make sense of it all at once.

Read the names of the hexagrams and the words of the text as an answer to your question. They almost always will be; very occasionally, the reading may be telling you something more urgent, but it's best to start by assuming that Yi has answered your question directly.

NAVIGATING THE TEXT

As you read your hexagrams and lines, you'll find some parts are in italic text and quotation marks. These are the words of the Yijing itself; everything else is only my commentary. What I have written about each hexagram and line is the heart of what I've found it to mean, but it is not the limit of what Yi can say to you in its own words.

Key Questions: some things the oracle might be asking *you* with this response.

Oracle: the voice of the hexagram as a whole.

Image, Pair and Sequence contain excerpts from the Ten Wings that are especially helpful in divination. The Image shows the hexagram as a landscape and relationship of trigrams, and is a good source of overall advice. The Pair and Sequence suggest how your answer is part of a larger process.

Lines: if your reading has changing lines, their associated texts show exactly where you stand (or might choose to stand) in relation to the hexagram as a whole.

HOW THE PARTS OF YOUR READING WORK TOGETHER

The key to understanding a reading is to know your way round its main components, how they fit together, and the different roles they play. If your reading includes changing lines, then you will need to understand primary hexagram, relating hexagram and changing lines together.

The two hexagrams, in conversation with one another, map out your whole answer. The primary hexagram shows you quite directly what your answer involves. The relating hexagram generally describes what the answer is about *for you*. It sets the primary hexagram in a broader context – an influence, a direction of travel, an underlying issue – that has to do with you and your relationship to it all.

If the two hexagrams map out a landscape for you, then the changing lines stick a pin in that map to say 'You are here!' – or at least, 'Here are some places you may find yourself.' They are the immediate answer to your question: as the most specific, focused part of a reading, their message always takes precedence over all other elements. (For example, the primary hexagram might describe a reassuringly secure situation, but a changing line could warn how insecure your position is within it.)

UNDERSTANDING CHANGING LINES

You can understand groups of changing lines that seem to contradict one another by setting their different messages in context. For example:

Lines tell a story Lines that can't all be true at once can still be true one after the other. You may find as you read through that the lowest line, where the story begins, is immediately recognizable, while the higher ones feel like more remote possibilities.

Lines show alternatives or choices Different lines may show you the outcomes of different courses of action.

Lines speak from different places The different line positions can correspond to layers of experience or awareness within a situation, and express their different perspectives:

Line 6: Beyond the main action, reviewing experience, asking what comes next
Line 5: Strength and self-determination, clear vision, being in command
Line 4: The capacity for action, asking how the work can be done
Line 3: An emerging identity, facing a transition – with fear or desire, resolution or indecision
Line 2: The heart's perception, the emotional centre, where you make and feel connections
Line 1: Inklings, just beginning to sense what could be involved or needed.

These can represent different individuals, and they can also represent or advise different parts of your self: we each have a community of 'inner selves' trying to make themselves heard.

TIPS FOR UNDERSTANDING THE LANGUAGE OF THE ORACLE

When the reading refers to people, these can be other people, or they can be parts of yourself. For example, 'small people' can be the voices of your smaller self, or people you meet, or both.

Yi uses gender primarily to describe roles in a situation. A woman can act like a male general; a man can have a 'woman's constancy'. (The original Chinese text doesn't usually identify gender at all. Of course, the English version and commentary has to choose either 'he' or 'she', but you can substitute whichever applies.)

A LITTLE HISTORICAL BACKGROUND

Among the many stories of change that weave through the Yijing, the clearest is that of the Zhou people. Many hexagrams allude to it, assuming the reader will know the story.

The Yi was first written down at a time of great upheaval, when the moral, economic and spiritual order of the land had disintegrated under the rule of the Shang dynasty. The Shang, the ruling family in China for 600 years, had fallen into corruption and forfeited Heaven's Mandate to rule. The Mandate is a calling and a blessing that comes from the highest spiritual power; it means both 'orders' and 'destiny'. King Wen of the Zhou, the 'Pattern King', developed and cultivated his realm and became fit to receive

the Mandate. After many years of preparation, Wen died at the garrison city of Feng. His son Wu, the 'Martial', led the armies on from Feng and across the great river to overthrow the Shang, founding a dynasty that was to endure almost 800 years.

INTEGRATING

This is the most important part of divination, when you establish the reading as an enduring part of your life: it's what makes the Yijing a 'Book of Change' and not just a 'Book of Nice Ideas'.

Integrating a reading means asking yourself specific, practical questions about how different parts of a reading apply and what you'll be doing about them. It also means absorbing it deeply, letting its images and advice shift your awareness. Integrating readings into ordinary life means enriching the ordinary with the extraordinary – not removing the extraordinary from the reading.

RECORD YOUR READING

For your readings to make the greatest difference in your life – individually and together – it's good to keep them in a journal. This is a way to give your readings more time and thought, and to watch how readings unfold as a conversation; it also becomes a priceless record of personal divination experience. Whether you use a computer or pen and paper, I suggest you create a journal format in which you can look up readings by topic, date and hexagram.

WAYS TO TAKE IT WITH YOU

You may act on a reading at once – or you may need to keep it in mind for a while. Here are a few suggested ways you could take a reading with you:

- Summarize the message you're taking from your reading in a phrase or two
- Memorize this and use it to challenge and re-route your inner conversations
- Draw, collage or mind-map the reading's images and themes
- Ensure you'll be reminded of your reading: draw the hexagram on a business card to take with you, set it as your computer's screensaver, pin it to the fridge, and so on.

ABOVE ALL...

Enjoy the oracle! May it give you all the illumination, challenge and sheer wonder it has given me and millions of others. I wish you the joy of discovery and realization in every part of your life.

MORE HELP WITH YOUR I CHING READINGS

For more help with your own readings, and free downloads including an example of a complete reading visit www.IChingReadings.com.

Key to the Hexagrams

Lower trigram		Qian	Zhen	Kan	Gen	Kun	Xun	Li	Dui
Qian		1	34	5	26	11	9	14	43
Zhen		25	51	3	27	24	42	21	17
Kan		6	40	29	4	7	59	64	47
Gen		33	62	39	52	15	53	56	31
Kun		12	16	8	23	2	20	35	45
Xun		44	32	48	18	46	57	50	28
Li		13	55	63	22	36	37	30	49
Dui		10	54	60	41	19	61	38	58

Hexagram 1, *Creative Force*

Key Questions

How can you liberate creative energy?
What wants to be created?

Oracle

'Creative Force.
From the source, creating success.
Constancy bears fruit.'

This is the pure creative spirit that flows through people and events: it drives towards manifestation, an inspiration that wants to be realized.

It begins with an opening to the source of the creative impulse – not plans or intentions, but the vital energy that powers them. Then you create success by sustaining a continuous, two-way flow between source and action. You step into the heart of a process of creation, welcome its momentum and find ways to join and work with it.

Through constancy, this brings out intrinsic potential and yields a harvest of positive results. To be constant is to be true to your intent, faithfully aligning all your choices with your original vision, and carrying your understanding through in practice and over time.

Image

'The heavens move ceaselessly.
A noble one in his own strength does not pause.'

Creative force is the absolute power of heaven, that moves the stars in their courses and makes the seasons turn. A noble one finds this creative force is within him, as close as his own breath. It does not need to pause and rest, and nor does he.

Pair

Hexagram 1 is paired and contrasted with Hexagram 2, creative Heaven with the receptive Earth. They are the cosmic father and mother.

'Creative Force is firm, the Earth is open.'

Hexagram 1 has six firm, yang lines; Hexagram 2 has six open, yin lines. The two together bring the world into being: idea and work, outpouring and receiving, inspiration and manifestation. Hexagram 1 marks a time for pure creativity, rather than for questions about what might be possible in practice.

CHANGING LINES

Line 1 *'Dragon underwater – don't act.'*

During the winter, the Chinese dragon sleeps at the bottom of a mountain lake. Until the dragon wakes in spring and flies out over the fields bringing rain, there can be no useful action.

Meanwhile, the dragon is invisible: a powerful energy is still hidden away, unable to play any active part. It may be obvious that the dragon is still dormant: that people are not personally ready, an idea is not sufficiently developed, or just that there is no field yet for action.

But even if it does seem possible to use this power, now is not the time. There's no way of knowing the nature of this change that's waiting in the depths, but it will probably not be mild or comfortable when it does emerge. To act now, as if you could plan out what's to come, would show a damaging lack of respect both for the stored potential of what could be, and for what already is.

Line 2 *'See the dragon in the fields.*
Fruitful to see great people.'

The dragon emerges into the expansive field of possibilities. You are called on to see the huge creative potential here, ready for you to work with.

Seeing great people may mean seeking out those who can provide information and guidance to help you make the most of this potential. It can also mean cultivating a clear inner vision of how it can be fulfilled, in real human relationships – recognizing greatness, and seeking to live up to it.

You need to see both the dragon and the great person: both where the present potential is, and what you have to aim for.

Line 3 *'Noble one creates and creates to the end of the day,*
At nightfall on the alert, as if in danger.
No mistake.'

This is a time of incessant creative activity – accelerated personal change, or just sheer unrelenting hard work. The Creative Force never rests, so when you are driven by it, neither do you.

These are hectic preparations for a possible transition: possibilities could be realized, the potential could take flight into reality, if only you can do enough now. So you create all day, and then at night you are still on the alert for all the factors you might not have seen. You're constantly aware that you might be walking with powers beyond your capacity. Yet although there's very little you can be sure of, your unceasing work and alertness mean you can avoid mistakes.

Line 4 *'Someone dancing in the abyss.*
No mistake.'

A mysterious, fluid moment: someone could be dancing in the abyss. Will the dragon take flight? For now, there is the dance along the border between 'just enough' and 'not quite there', stretching your wings and playing with vast possibilities. There's no shortage of creative drive and imagination, but it's not clear what will prove attainable. Whatever the outcome, the dance is a key part of the process of creation, and no mistake.

Line 5 *'Dragon flying in heaven.*
Fruitful to see great people.'

The dragon is in full flight, creative force released into full expression. Clouds follow him and the crops will grow. It is the right time and place to act.

Now the whole creative force is available, it's all the more important to see great people, whether with inner or outer vision – to lend direction to the power available, and to realize it on the ground in real, human ways.

Line 6 *'Overweening dragon has regrets.'*

There comes a time when even dragons need to recognize the limits and fly a little lower. This one is too confident and too loud, soaring onward and upward as if he need never come down. He neglects to pay attention to what supports his flight, and sends out all the wrong messages. The consequences will be regrettable.

All lines changing *'See a flock of dragons with no leader. Good fortune.'*

With every line changing, the totality of creative drive opens out into all the fields of possibility. All the dragons are in flight. There's no need to take the lead to guide this to a successful conclusion: you need only allow the whole creative force to come through, where there is space for the best outcome to grow by itself.

Hexagram 2, *Earth*

Key Questions

How are you being guided?
How can you lend your strength?

Oracle

'Earth.
From the source, creating success.
The constancy of a mare bears fruit.
A noble one has a direction to go.
At first, confusion. Later, gains a master.
Fruitful in the southwest, gaining partners.
In the northeast, losing partners.
Peaceful constancy brings good fortune.'

Earth is first described in the same words as the Creative Force of Hexagram 1 because they are partners in the flow of creation. Creation unfolds from the original vital energy, creating success with an ongoing exchange between spirit and daily work, flowing through to fruition – in Earth, through the constancy of a mare.

The mare is strong, tireless and incomparably fast, and she is acutely sensitive to the subtlest cues. When you have a mare's constancy, you will be steadily loyal to the truth, and always alert and responsive to guidance.

The noble one has a direction to go: she is purposeful, she has a destination in mind, but this doesn't mean she has her route to it already mapped out. And so at first there is confusion: you set out like a pioneer, open to all the possibilities, and find them as many as scattered rice-grains. But later, since you have set yourself in motion, you can receive guidance – you 'gain a master'.

A master is someone who lights the way. You gain someone or something to be loyal to, where you can find fulfilment in service. Once you have this guiding principle (which may or may not be a person), you begin to follow signs as fluently as the mare.

The Zhou people sought out allies in the southwest before venturing into the northeast to face the Shang. There is a balance to be found between joining with like-minded people and following your own calling alone – but gaining allies comes first. Perhaps your individual sense of purpose emerges more strongly when you've learned to work responsively with others, like the mare running with the herd.

And when you can spread your senses out to roam southwest and northeast without limit, you will be peacefully at home in the whole earth.

Image

'*Power of the land: Earth.
A noble one, with generous character, carries all the beings.*'

Through the power of the land, Earth is heaven's partner in bringing the world into being. The sun needs a place to shine, rain a place to fall, and seeds need soil to grow in; flashes of inspiration need space and time to expand and take shape; great ideas need work to be realized.

The power of the land is to provide everything needed for all things to find their shape. A noble one embodies this power in the deep generosity of her character. She certainly need never worry about the limits of her strength.

CHANGING LINES

Line 1 '*Treading on frost,
Hard ice is arriving.*'

When you feel the first hints of frost underfoot, you know the seasons are turning and hard ice must follow. What you are noticing now are the first subtle signs that reveal the way of things. Read them with great sensitivity, and you can see the pattern of what is to come.

The way you walk now will help to harden the ice into a smooth path. Tiny changes now determine where you will find yourself once the ice has hardened. Where are you making your home for the winter?

Line 2 '*Surveying the realms' greatness.
Without rehearsal, there is nothing that does not bear fruit.*'

Now you have a clear view of your 'direction to go', far across the realms of possibility and imagination. What grows in these strange fields is not anything you could plan for, and may not be anything you envisage. Hence there is nothing to learn, practise or train for: better to leave all possibilities open than narrow them down by preparing for one particular outcome.

The important thing is not how you prepare, but what guides you, far beyond what you can see now. Whatever materializes, this will bear fruit.

Line 3 '*Containing a thing of beauty: this allows constancy.
Maybe following a king's work –*'

Without accomplishment, there is completion.'

There is an inner treasure here, already whole and complete in itself, needing nothing added. You can stay true to it without concerning yourself with immediate personal achievement.

So even as you work, perhaps to realize that inner potential, you know that winning something to show for your efforts now is not so important; it's sufficient that the work be completed in the end.

Line 4 *'Tied up in a bag.*
No blame, no praise.'

The nature of the situation is hidden away from your scrutiny, beyond 'blame' or 'praise': you cannot evaluate it, nor can you intervene to help things along. Maybe this is not something you need to know; maybe it would be better not to expose yourself to evaluation either. Don't ask how to act on your emotions and imaginings – just wrap them up, embrace and allow them all, and let things be.

Line 5 *'Yellow lower garments.*
From the source, good fortune.'

Yellow is the colour of the good Chinese soil, and the colour of the skirts of young noblemen. So wearing yellow symbolizes a deliberate choice to put on the qualities of earth: open, responsive, generous and unobtrusive. It quietly demonstrates your readiness to relinquish control and be of service.

Line 6 *'Dragons battling in the wilds.*
Their blood black and yellow.'

The power of earth lies in being constantly open to all possibilities. At the extreme, this becomes sheer inertia, resisting the creative impulse that would give a new and specific shape to things. Such change is at once necessary and unthinkable. And so earth's dragon battles with heaven's dragon, and the energy of both heaven and earth drains away through their wounds. This battle can be played out between people, or as an individual's inner struggle.

All lines changing *'Ever-flowing constancy bears fruit.'*

With this reading, every line of Hexagram 2 is wide open for change; earth is so actively receptive as to become transparent to the creative force that seeks expression through it. This is a major change; it takes a long time and much loyal persistence for it to come to fruition. Being constant now is like swimming in the creative flow as it flows on past frustrations and obstacles.

Hexagram 3, *Sprouting*

Key Questions

What is beginning?
Where is the growing centre, and
where can you find help for it?

Oracle

'Sprouting.
From the source, creating success, constancy bears fruit.
Don't use this to have a direction to go,
Fruitful to establish feudal lords.'

Sprouting is the very beginning: a growing centre, putting out roots into the unknown and breaking through the hard soil. Inner life reaches out into the world, experiencing resistance for the first time. The creative drive of heaven and earth joins together and grows. It's tiny, scarcely born, but burgeoning with life and a great desire to attain full growth.

It's far too early yet to narrow all the possibilities down to a single destination. Just as a plant sends out roots in all directions, a new ruler needs to set up a network of feudal lords. These are an image for helpers, human or otherwise: everything that brings you support and expands your sphere of awareness and influence. In exploring all possibilities, you enrich and strengthen the centre as growth begins.

Image

'Clouds, thunder: Sprouting.
A noble one weaves warp and weft.'

At the beginning, clouds and thunder swirl together in a creative ferment. The creative impulse rises like thunder and flows out into the world's confusion.

The word for warp threads also means a canonical text and a channel where energy flows. These are the first principles: you can weave all the colours of experience into the structure they provide, translating creative chaos into a creative order.

Sequence

'There is heaven and earth, and so the ten thousand things are born.
Overflowing the space between heaven and earth, the ten thousand things.
And so Sprouting follows: Sprouting means filling to overflowing;
Sprouting means the beginning of things' birth.'

The Sequence of the hexagrams is born here, from heaven and earth (Hexagrams 1 and 2). This is a time of intense, overwhelming creativity.

Pair

Sprouting forms a pair with Hexagram 4, Not Knowing:

'Sprouting: seeing, and not letting go your dwelling place.
Not knowing: disordered and also clear.'

You are like a new king, surveying the realm without leaving his home at its centre. Or you are like an infant, who contemplates the world from the security of her cradle. Staying centred, you always know where you are. There will be time later to discover how much you don't know.

CHANGING LINES

Line 1 *'Encircled by stones.*
            Fruitful to settle with constancy,
            Fruitful to establish feudal lords.'

At the very beginning, you're hemmed in by obstacles all around you. You can't forge ahead as directly as you would like, yet you still want to come into harmony with your environment. So instead of feeling trapped here, put down roots and make yourself at home. Reach out: expand your awareness beyond the obstacles, and make connections that can help you.

Line 2 *'Now sprouting, now hesitating, now driving a team of horses.*
            Not robbers at all, but marital allies.
            The child-woman's constancy – no children.
            Ten years go by, then there are children.'

The suitor drives out to the house of his betrothed with a full team of horses. Even if at first he looks

like a robber, he comes to enrich the bride and her people, not to take anything away from her. And yet … this is such an early stage. The bride will not be old enough to have children for years to come.

You need to grow beyond your current limits, and you're drawn to partnership and commitment as a powerful way to do so. There is a genuine opportunity here, but it's natural to hesitate before accepting. Constancy in a time of sprouting means honouring the youth of young things, and making agreements that fit well with the natural pace of their growth. This is all part of a very long-term process. You might ask yourself whether you want to enter into a commitment that will take so long to come to fruition – or whether the partnership is a good fit for your own path of growth.

Line 3 *'Pursuing a stag with no forester,*
Simply entering into the centre of the forest.
A noble one reads the subtle signs and sets this aside.
Going on: shame.'

You're chasing after your desires with no guide, perhaps so entranced by anticipation that you forget where you are now – namely on the verge of getting humiliatingly lost. Instead of expanding your awareness from the centre, you're letting your desires get ahead of you and plunging into the unknown.

There is still time to recognize where this is leading you and desist. If you're in this for the long term, there's no need for such haste.

Line 4 *'Driving a full team of horses, seeking marital alliance.*
Going on, good fortune - nothing that does not bear fruit.'

The suitor drives out to seek his future bride. If he carries on, he will enjoy good fortune, and everything he does will bear fruit. This is not a time to fixate on 'getting' something and being recognized. It's an adventure: striving for growth through partnership, wholeheartedly embracing the new. By harnessing the energy of the moment in this way, you can reap a harvest from everything you encounter.

Line 5 *'Sprouting's juice.*
Small constancy, good fortune - great constancy, pitfall.'

The seedling draws nourishment from its roots to revitalize its growth. Such rich energy is best used with loyalty to yourself and to principle – with a constancy fitting for the open, innovative spirit of the time. Small constancy stays true to the idea, but is flexible about the way forward, finding the lines of least resistance through intelligent sensitivity to the environment. Great constancy insists on implementing the idea as envisaged; it knows the way, and nothing else will do.

Young plants use their energy to grow soft leaves and stems, not solid trunks.

Line 6 *'Now driving a team of horses, now tears of blood flow.'*

The suitor drives out with his best horses, but there is no bride here for him to find. Pouring out the best of yourself in a concerted effort to forge ahead, you find no response, and your energy drains away. You're over-extended, too narrowly focused on a single direction, and forgetting what a well-rooted relationship feels like.

Hexagram 4, *Not Knowing*

Key Questions

What don't you know?
What if you didn't need to know all the answers now?
How can you learn from experience?

Oracle

'Not knowing, creating success.
I do not seek the young ignoramus, the young ignoramus seeks me.
The first consultation speaks clearly.
The second and third pollute the waters,
Polluted, and hence not speaking.
Constancy bears fruit.'

Not Knowing literally means being covered over, like a young animal hidden away in the undergrowth by its mother. So you are ignorant, and cannot see as far as you would like to – but this is not such a terrible thing while you are still so small. To be small and ignorant is a creative, harmonious way to engage with your world, and holding steadily to not knowing – and hence to learning – will bring good results.

But this flow, from 'creating success' to 'constancy bears fruit', is interrupted when the young ignoramus goes running after answers, as if it were embarrassing not to know. In his anxious persistence he shows a profound disrespect – for his teacher, and also for the answer he is seeking that he imagines can be had so quickly. So the 'I' who speaks here gives one clear answer, and then may refuse to answer – or perhaps there is just such confusion that no answers can be understood.

That speaker can be another person you're asking for a response you need. It can also be the oracle itself, or what speaks through it.

Image

'Below the mountain, spring water comes forth: Not Knowing.
A noble one nourishes character with the fruits of action.'

The pure spring rises under the shelter of the mountain; it doesn't know where it's going, yet its flow becomes steadily deeper and stronger. In the same way, a noble one nurtures personal character and strength with the fruits of going forward and taking action. Learning comes from experience, not in the form of ready-made answers.

Sequence

Not Knowing follows from Hexagram 3, Sprouting:

'Things that are newly born must needs be ignorant, and so Not Knowing follows. Not Knowing means ignorance, and the youth of things.'

You are at an early stage of development, like an infant just beginning to toddle out into the wider world. Suddenly, you find yourself ignorant; the world is a much less orderly place than it appeared from the cradle. So if you have a confused sense of losing your centre, this is a sign that you're seeing the real world more clearly than before.

CHANGING LINES

Line 1   *'Sending out the ignoramus,*
Fruitful to make use of punishing people,
To make use of loosening fetters and manacles.
Going on in that way is shameful.'

Sent out into the confusion of the world, the ignoramus will learn best by experiencing all the consequences of his actions to the full. You need to be free to hear the truth; the only experience you can really learn from is a direct and unfettered one. A first step to learning is to let go of everything that shackles you – which might include ideas, rules and over-complicated conditions. It may be hard to relinquish these, especially if they mean you 'know where you are'. However, if you always know where you are, you can never get anywhere or learn anything. It is shameful to live in fetters.

Line 2   *'Embracing the ignoramus, good fortune.*
Receiving the woman, good fortune.
The child governs the home.'

Embrace the ignoramus – or your own ignorance – like a child in the womb: accept it, hold it, allow it to be as it is. Make the experience of not knowing an integral part of yourself, and you can start learning, which is good fortune.

27

Similarly, be like a young man who receives a wife into his home: open up your world to the possibility of new life, and growth, and unpredictable things beyond your experience. Not knowing allows growth, which is also good fortune.

Then the known ways of doing things, those well-established frameworks you have depended on, are stripped away; you lose all sense of being the adult in charge. Instead, you allow the child, the natural learner, to govern your space and lead through not knowing – though Yi doesn't say how well the home will be governed.

Line 3 *'Don't take this woman.*
She sees a man of bronze, and there is no self.
No direction bears fruit.'

Don't take this woman: don't join yourself to a person who behaves like this, and don't adopt this mentality as your own. She sees her prospective partner as if he were made of bronze, not flesh and blood, casting him in the mould of her ideas and what she already (supposedly) knows. Needing everything to fit this gleaming image and follow predetermined patterns, she cannot relate to him as a real human being, and loses her own sense of self. Such inauthenticity means there is no direction you could usefully pursue or explore.

Line 4 *'Confined ignoramus - shame.'*

The ignoramus is confined; not knowing becomes a trap. How are you to learn anything if there are walls separating you from other people? You need to overcome your insecurity and reach out – maybe even before you know what you will encounter. Staying in confinement would be shameful.

Line 5 *'Young ignoramus - good fortune.'*

The Oracle identifies the young ignoramus as the one who seeks answers. He enjoys good fortune because of his youthful, energetic constancy and because there is nothing to impede the flow of his learning. He owns no stockpile of ready-made answers, and has no preconceptions between him and the truth.

Line 6 *'Striking the ignoramus.*
Fruitless to act like an enemy,
Fruitful to resist enmity.'

You are striking out at ignorance – your own, or someone else's. This might work for the Zen master who clouts his students to wake them up – but not as an attack that makes the ignoramus the enemy. If you are attacking another person, you will injure your way of communication; if you are being self-critical and applying self-discipline, then you are dividing yourself into two opposing forces and becoming your own enemy.

You may well feel impatient and frustrated with not knowing, and strongly motivated to do something about it. That can bear fruit, but not if you act in a small-minded, reactive way – only if you bear the learner's full potential in mind, and actively protect him from hostility and isolation.

Hexagram 5, *Waiting*

Key Questions

How can you wait patiently and with commitment?
While you wait, how can you best make yourself ready?

Oracle

*'Waiting, with truth and confidence.
Shining out, creating success: constancy brings good fortune.
Fruitful to cross the great river.'*

You wait for what you need, like a farmer waiting for the weather to change. This is not a passive state; you can dance for rain, influence events by bringing yourself into harmony with the outcome you need. But you cannot force this, you can only attend to it. You will need patience: it may all take much longer than you had imagined.

When you are fully present in waiting, your intense attention shines out like a beacon, beginning a creative engagement with the world – not by working on anything, but by waiting on it and holding your faith.

And in crossing the river, committing yourself to go as far as you can towards what you're waiting for, you begin the transition into the world where it is real.

Image

*'The clouds are above heaven: Waiting.
A noble one eats, drinks and relaxes with music.'*

A noble one doesn't hover anxiously in the doorway watching the skies; instead, with sureness and constancy in his heart, and fluidity in his actions, he thrives in the present moment.

Feasting when you can't cultivate your fields shows confidence, and it keeps you rested and prepared for the moment when you can act. In ancient China, where the ancestral spirits helped to bring better weather, you would invite them to share your meals, revitalizing your relationship with what provides for you.

Sequence

Waiting follows from Hexagram 4, Not Knowing:

'Young things cannot do without nourishment, and so Waiting follows. Waiting means the way of eating and drinking.'

Naturally, young things don't spring instantly into a state of full growth – and nor does wisdom, or Knowing. They must be nourished patiently over time.

Pair

Waiting forms a pair with Hexagram 6, Arguing:

'Waiting means no progress, Arguing means no connection.'

Lacking what you need, you could challenge the injustice and Argue your case; or Wait and have faith. Though you're not moving forward, you might be inviting help and connection.

CHANGING LINES

Line 1 *'Waiting at the outskirts altar,*
Fruitful to use perseverance – no mistake.'
Outside the town walls is a simple altar-mound, where people gather to make offerings for a good harvest. You need these wider spaces with longer views. Don't rush to the centre of the action to take the initiative, or focus exclusively on a single issue. Only by seeing your desire as a small part of the larger landscape can you see the potential for it to be realized.

Even when nothing works and you start to think of giving up, don't lose sight of this potential. Always act in a way that invites the possibility nearer; always hold it in connection with that larger reality; be utterly consistent.

Line 2 *'Waiting on the sands, there are small words.*
In the end, good fortune.'
The situation is insecure, in a state of flux, like sand shifting under your feet. Now you're committed to a course of action, you have to wait to see what – if anything – will come of it. There's no solid feedback to tell you where you stand, and you feel very exposed.

The small mind hurries to fill the space with very 'small' talk – yours, or other people's. It voices doubts and reacts to insecurity with pettiness. But this shouldn't distract you from your Waiting. You've already got things underway in a good direction; you're not stuck here. In the long run, there will be good fortune.

Line 3 *'Waiting in the bog invites the arrival of robbers.'*

A bog is not a healthy place to wait – and yet your wagon is sinking in up to its axles while you wait to get the measure of things. Perhaps you feel that you must have it all under control – especially your expectations – for fear of further suffering.

Yet sitting here makes you vulnerable – to unscrupulous people who take advantage of your inability to move, and to your own lesser self. When you don't expect to make progress, negativity arises: impatience, guilt, the creeping loss of hope, and arguments about how things *should* be done.

Line 4 *'Waiting in blood.*
Come out of the pit.'

You may need to wait, but you do not need to wait here, in this cramped pit of dark emotions, where hope and vitality drain away through many wounds. The longer you live here, the more you feel helpless to change anything; you start to forget the world beyond the pit. You may imagine you are proving something by never abandoning your post, no matter how much you (and others) bleed.

Do whatever it takes to change your state. Let yourself be guided out of your pit; don't allow the painful experience to define you. How could you see anything in its true perspective from the bottom of a hole?

Line 5 *'Waiting with food and drink.*
Constancy, good fortune.'

It all takes much longer than you imagined, and you're not in a position to dictate a faster pace. Sometimes the best way to be true to your vision is simply to rest and recuperate for the journey.

That means taking pleasure in this moment and not postponing your happiness. Make the investment to replenish relationships; create opportunities for freer, more harmonious communication. When you are well nourished, you can wait without tiring: you can be constant, which brings good fortune.

Line 6 *'Entering into the pit.*
There are uninvited guests - three people come.
Honour them: in the end, good fortune.'

Inside your own small space, where you wait quietly and in stillness, several guests will come. These 'guests' may be unexpected encounters, unusual opportunities, or strange truths. They're certainly not recognizable as what you were waiting for; they may be something you never asked for, and perhaps you would prefer to send them all on their way.

However, there are stories of unexpected visitors who turn out to be gods in disguise, and reward those who welcome them. So work with what you are given; instead of gazing fixedly at the horizon, waiting for what you had in mind, go inside and wait on your guests. Make space for them to stay for a while, sit at their feet and listen.

Hexagram 6, *Arguing*

Key Questions

What are you arguing for?
If you can't win this one, what else can you do?

Oracle

'Arguing.
There is truth and confidence, blocked.
Vigilant and centred, good fortune. Ending, pitfall.
Fruitful to see great people,
Fruitless to cross the great river.'

You argue for what you need – for sustenance, or to be believed, or simply for justice – for you know in your bones that things are not as they should be. Yet no matter how deep and true your convictions, you find yourself frustrated, and your sense of being in resonance and connected with the world is choked off. It's important, now, to centre yourself in vigilance – in a heart open and alert to all the potentials for change, so you stay poised and capable of responsive movement in any direction. To freeze into a combative, defiant posture, holding onto your sense of wrongness to the bitter end, would not resolve conflict but only establish it in perpetuity.

When frustrated and blocked, you need to see great people – those whose higher perspective enables them to see beyond the argument to a larger truth. Perhaps you can find that shift in perspective within yourself; perhaps you need to consult with someone wiser, who is outside the conflict. Meanwhile, it's fruitless to commit yourself further to your position out of sheer defiance.

Image

'Heaven joins with stream, contradictory movements: Arguing.
A noble one, starting work, plans how to begin.'

Water flows downhill, away from heaven. Your inner momentum diverges from the immutable laws, pulled away by the flow of emotion: you're in dispute with *how it is*. This dissenting impulse inspires you to 'start work' and take action. Arguing makes for much better beginnings than endings. In order

to direct the inner momentum intelligently, without worsening the conflict, a noble one thinks of heaven joining with the stream; he plans from the outset how to bring the emotional currents of commitment back into accord with absolute principles.

Sequence

Arguing follows from Hexagram 5, Waiting:

'Drinking and eating naturally mean Arguing.'

When our needs and appetites are involved, we will fight – and when we Argue, need and the fear of lack probably motivate us. Hexagram 5 Waits for what it needs; Hexagram 6 demands it.

CHANGING LINES

Line 1 *'Not a lasting place for work.*
There are small words.
Ending, good fortune.'

You cannot do useful work here; activity goes against the current, and will not achieve the results you're looking for. You've yet to locate the area that really needs your attention. Instead, lots of small words in inner or outer conversations keep you preoccupied with small things, anxiously seeking security, setting up a flurry of chattering debate that distracts from the bigger (and often much simpler) issue.

Although *major* conflict cannot just be 'ended' – it needs resolving at a higher level – these small-scale wranglings can be quietly rounded off. You can move on in search of your real inspiration, and leave small things behind.

Line 2 *'Cannot master this argument,*
Return home, escape to your town's people,
Three hundred households.
No blunder.'

No matter how long you fight on, this is an argument you can't possibly win. The only way to escape the frustrating standstill is to leave it behind and go home.

Your home is the place, and the people, that offer you refuge, acceptance and enough support. It's good to remember that there is a modest, ordinary world outside the bubble of conflict with resources and connections of its own – it takes some of the urgency and panic out of your arguing. Return, reconnect, see a less abstract picture, and you can avoid some serious mistakes.

Line 3 *'Feeding on ancient power and virtue.*
Constancy: danger. Ending, good fortune.
Maybe following a king's work,
Without accomplishment.'

You feed yourself on power that comes from the past – maybe strong personal values, or deep instinctual strengths, or the qualities of ancient heroes. This is potent nourishment: the only question is how or where it might find a place in your life now. If you let it feed your energy for arguing, and keep on trying to shape the world to fit with ancient virtue, you're likely to run into trouble and get hurt.

It's better to allow the ancient story to be complete in itself, instead of fighting to realize it here and now. You can still incorporate it as an inner source of strength, far deeper and more powerful than mere righteous indignation, and then get on quietly with the business at hand. If that involves working towards an objective, you shouldn't expect great achievements or recognition – but when you are well nourished on ancient power and virtue, you won't need such things.

Line 4 *'Cannot master this argument,*
Returning and taking up the mandate.
With a change of heart, peaceful constancy is good fortune.'

You can't win here – there's nothing for you in this argument. So step outside it – can you see a wider perspective, beyond the positions the conflict defines for you? Turn away from arguing and towards your own purpose here. When you rediscover the sense of being drawn to do something, you recapture your motivation along with it: not being able to win an argument does not mean being powerless. Instead of wasting your energy in struggle, you can go your way with constancy, at peace with how things are.

Line 5 *'Arguing: good fortune from the source.'*

This is a different kind of arguing. Instead of committing yourself to a position and digging in to defend it to the end, you argue for the sake of understanding the truth. (And you're well aware that 'the end' is only found in fiction.) Arguing because you *haven't* decided your position, you're better placed to make perceptive choices and work out the best way forward for everyone involved. Trust yourself: you will be able to recognize the way when you see it, because your vision transcends the arguments. Meanwhile, you have truths to seek and aspirations to follow, so make yourself heard.

Line 6 *'Maybe awarded a grand leather belt.*
By the end of the day, stripped of it three times.'

Someone wins the argument! And then the victor's prize is taken away again – and again, and again – because there is no such thing as a final victory. This is not the way to leave Arguing behind; it's the way to trap yourself in a struggle for scraps, constantly hampered by the fear of loss. If all you aim for is a 'win', then expect it to be followed by losses. Change happens.

Hexagram 7, *the Army*

Key Questions

What are you aiming for?
How can you get more from your strengths?
With all your efforts, are you creating the life you want?

Oracle

'The Army: with constancy.
Mature people, good fortune – no mistake.'

When there is cause, the ruler raises an army. This is a time when *everything* revolves around a central objective: inner and outer resources are realigned and ordered in accordance with it. It's important that a mature leader take responsibility, not least so that intensity of focus does not become blinkered vision or pure belligerence, turning everything that is not the goal into the enemy.

Balancing the drive to 'get it done' with a measured, disciplined approach allows you to achieve your objective effectively and with less 'collateral damage': good fortune, without mistake.

Image

'In the centre of the earth is a stream: the Army.
A noble one accepts the people and gathers together crowds.'

The stream within the earth flows strongly because the earth accepts and absorbs all the water that falls on it; a noble one builds an army with the same open acceptance. You can find your greatest strength in the flow of your *whole* self – by recruiting all your different character traits and hidden, underground emotions.

Sequence

The Army follows from Hexagram 6, Arguing:

'Arguing naturally means that crowds rise up, and so the Army follows. The Army means crowds.'

First you react with indignation against the status quo; then you begin to organize a way to change it. 'Crowds' of people, energies and resources gather around that original focal point of grievance. The emotions that began as mere reactive indignation become an inner reserve of strength.

Pair

The Army forms a pair with Hexagram 8, Seeking Union:

'Seeking Union means delight; the Army means grieving.'

The choices of Seeking Union are made freely, following natural affinity, as the streams flow together over the earth. Those of the Army – whose work is needed to prepare for Seeking Union – are driven by necessity: the ends must justify the means. When the army marches on its objective, look out for casualties and ruined fields.

CHANGING LINES

Line 1 *'The army sets out according to pitch-pipes,*
At odds with the strength of the army – pitfall.'

Pitch-pipes are used like drums, to create concerted, disciplined movement: as the army gathers its power and moves forward, it's important to ensure that all actions are in harmony with the goal. Yet it's equally important that the goal itself – however attractive – should be in harmony with your own nature and strengths. If strength and purpose fail to communicate and resonate together at this early stage, it all falls apart.

Line 2 *'Positioned in the centre of the army.*
Good fortune, no mistake.
The king issues a mandate three times.'

The 'mature person' of the Oracle becomes the leader, bringing 'good fortune, no mistake'. He doesn't supervise from a distance: he moves to the front lines, the midst of the action. This means he is in the best possible position to sense what is needed – and this is why the king sends him a mandate, or orders. Put yourself in this central position, consent to the responsibility, and the mandate will come: in a way, it is simply the outward sign of an inner agreement you have already made.

The mandate comes not once to this receptive leader, but three times. The strategy or the plans may need to change; don't assume that what you have in mind to do now will be the final word on the matter. This goes beyond your existing knowledge.

Line 3 *'Perhaps the army carts corpses – pitfall.'*
The corpses used to be filled with vitality, but now they're just dead weight.

The mindset, strategy or emotion that used to be an inspiring source of strength is now a lifeless husk. Time to lay it to rest; carting it with you will do you real harm.

Line 4 *'The army camps on the left – no mistake.'*
To camp on the left is to pull back to a position with an easy way of retreat. It is time for the army to stop, relax and recuperate. This is not a defeat or a surrender, but a pause to rethink. As the leader of your own campaign, you can safely free yourself for the moment from the necessity of marching onward, loosen your grip on command, and reconsider your strategies, directions and alliances.

Line 5 *'The fields have game.*
Fruitful to speak of capture – no mistake.
When the elder son leads the army,
And younger son carts corpses – constancy, pitfall.'
There is game for the hunt: there is an opportunity or opening or challenge, something waiting to be grasped; the stakes are real. You're in a responsible position and must engage, and yet you're surrounded by unknowns. It's no mistake to take the time to discuss strategy and gather intelligence.

There is an adult present to take charge, but there is also a rash, inexperienced youngster, who might be unnerved by the unpredictable. He carts corpses: he will not lay the past to rest, instead clinging to its patterns almost like a talisman. But this is a time for an authentic, commensurate response, not to go on automatic pilot.

Line 6 *'The great leader has a mandate*
To found a state and receive the households.
Don't use small people.'
The time for fighting is over; now the army's energies must be redirected into building a new world. A more open time is coming, founded on sincere relationships, and there is a profusion of tasks and challenges – all of them new. The task is no longer to pursue a known objective, but to lay the foundations for unknowable future growth. There is no longer any place for aggressive responses, or for people who are reactive and think small. Don't turn to such people; don't call on your own inner 'small person'.

Hexagram 8, *Seeking Union*

Key Questions

Where do you belong?
Is this a good fit?
Do you choose to join?

Oracle

'*Seeking union, good fortune.*
At the origin of oracle consultation,
From the source, ever-flowing constancy.
No mistake.
Not at rest, coming on all sides.
For the latecomer, pitfall.'

To seek union is to search for connection and belonging, discovering how it all fits together and creating a new world out of relationships.

It begins where divination begins: at your very source. Ask yourself why it was important to ask this question; get to know where you're coming from. When you find the source, you can flow perpetually out from there towards the right choices and connections. Such self-examination is not a mistake; it's the best way to avoid mistakes. It gives you and your relationships the authenticity of water, which flows together on the earth without changing its nature.

Seeking Union is natural, but not without stress. Singleness of purpose attracts restlessness (from within and without); demands are made on you from all directions at once. Not all the people or all the feelings that appear will be helpful.

Yu the Great conquered the Chinese floods through a lifetime of hard toil. When his work was complete and the land was safe, he summoned the lords and spirits to a meeting to found the new world. One of them, Fang Feng, came late; Yu had him executed.

To re-create a world of relationships, like Yu, is good fortune. To hesitate and come late, like Fang, is not. The decisive leader has to eliminate the non-committal spirit, the one who procrastinates and isn't quite sure whether to believe in this new union.

Image

'Above earth is the stream: Seeking Union.
The ancient kings founded countless cities for relationship with all the feudal lords.'

The streams flow together naturally over the earth; people, too, have their natural confluences. The ancient kings strengthened these by building cities – near the rivers, perhaps, following the contours of the landscape.

You can support and commit to your relationships in the same way, recognizing their natural flow and working with it.

Sequence

Seeking Union follows from Hexagram 7, the Army:

'Crowds naturally have occasion to Seek Union.'

First everything gathers around a single goal, and then there is a desire to connect and form relationships within the group. After the battles have been fought, it's time to start creating a new realm.

CHANGING LINES

Line 1 *'With truth and confidence, seeking union,*
No mistake.
With truth and confidence to overflow the vessel
An end comes – further good fortune.'

Seeking union begins with truth and confidence. There is a pure, almost childlike impulse towards relationship that springs from an overflowing sincerity and trust. No matter what happens next, it is not a mistake.

The 'end' that comes from this, bringing more good fortune, is a completion, a rounding-off, and also a beginning. True understanding grows from here.

Line 2 *'Seeking union's origin, inside.*
Constancy, good fortune.'

Union begins with your own natural affinities, and an inner, heart-felt impulse towards connection.

Holding steadily to this brings good fortune. This is very simple, and there is no need to complicate matters by trying to meet external standards or get external confirmation. Far more important to remember where *you* are coming from.

Line 3 *'Seeking union with non-people.'*

The desire to form relationships is very powerful, especially when you're struggling. So you look for allies somewhere different – but end up seeking union with people and ways of thinking that you cannot connect with. They cannot support you because they are not of your kind; you cannot join with them without denying your own nature.

Line 4 *'Outside, seeking union.*
Constancy, good fortune.'

Connecting with what's outside puts one's own experience in perspective. It's a relationship to something different, and to something *larger* – a bigger story, a broader view, something that expands and opens. To relate with steadiness of purpose to something outside your experience brings good fortune.

Line 5 *'A demonstration of seeking union:*
The king uses three beaters,
Lets the game in front go.
The city people are not coerced.
Good fortune.'

When the king hunts, he leaves a way open for the game to escape. Only those animals who spontaneously come towards him will be taken. He governs the city in the same way, without forcing people.

When you are seeking union, take charge like this king: go out into the field and look for the connections you want, be inviting and encouraging – and then leave the way open for people to choose their own direction. What's meant to come, will come.

Line 6 *'Seeking union without a head.*
Pitfall.'

Something essential is missing here. There is no commitment, no leadership, no chosen purpose. The process of relating and connecting carries on as if by rote, but with no clear idea of how it all applies on a real, personal level. This is no good. It's not enough to know where you're coming from; you need to choose where you're going.

Hexagram 9, *Small Taming*

Key Questions

What small thing can I work on today?
How can I cultivate a better terrain?

Oracle

'Small taming, creating success.
Dense clouds without rain
Come from my Western altars.'

To 'tame' is to restrain and also to accumulate and nurture: it's what the farmer does. Here, the small farmer cultivates the soil of his own small plot, hoping the offerings made at the Western altars will bring rain.

The Zhou people, like the clouds, came from the West. Before they were ready to receive the Mandate of Heaven and bring about change, they prepared for many decades, cultivating their society like earth.

So a time of Small Taming brings great hope for future growth and success – it's just that, at present, there is no rain, only clouds, and all they have brought so far is gloom. This means 'small restraint', the experience of small, frustrating setbacks and things that don't quite work yet.

However, this also brings advice to cultivate the situation and yourself in small ways, developing your readiness and fitness just as a small farmer works the soil. You can't make things grow in a single gesture, and so you need self-restraint: you have to work steadily, responding conscientiously to the realities here at ground level, caring for the small details.

Image

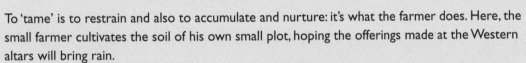

'Wind moves above heaven: Small Taming.
A noble one cultivates the natural pattern of character.'

The wind moves above heaven: it doesn't yet bring rain to earth. It is directed by the inner creative force of heaven, naturally moving with it.

Inwardly there are unchanging principles; outwardly, your actions gradually take on the shape of those inner principles. This is self-cultivation that aligns you with a creative power. It concentrates on growing potential rather than bringing about results.

Sequence

Small Taming follows from Hexagram 8, Seeking Union:

'Seeking union naturally has occasion to tame things, and so Small Taming follows.'

You have freely chosen where you belong and with whom, following your natural affinities. Now, if any of the potential you were drawn to is to be realized, you need to begin the detailed work. After the homesteader has entered virgin territory and chosen his own plot, he must get up next morning and every morning to work the soil, one weed at a time.

Pair

Small Taming forms a pair with Hexagram 10, Treading:

'Small Taming is solitary; Treading does not come to rest.'

Seeking to relate to the power that will make greater things possible, first you prepare alone and learn its nature, then you develop the capacity to move with it constantly.

CHANGING LINES

Line 1　　*'Returning to your own path,*
How could you be wrong?
Good fortune.'

When you hesitate about the right course of action, first come back to your starting point. Restore your sense of your own nature, where you come from and how you are rooted in the world; rediscover how your feet touch the earth. The right course of action, for you, is *your own path*. How could it be otherwise?

Line 2　　*'Drawn back, returning.*
Good fortune.'

To be 'drawn back' is like being an ox led by a rope. Circumstances make what you need to do quite clear. This pull – perhaps from the demands of relationships – can feel like an interference with your personal plans, but it is genuine guidance, leading you back to your own right path: you're blessed to receive it.

Line 3 *'A cart losing its wheel spokes.*
Husband and wife avert their eyes.'

Things come apart. The spokes are such a small component of the cart, yet when they are lost the whole system collapses. Husband and wife avoid one another's gaze: where you would expect communication and rapport, there is an inner disconnection.

There is more strain than the spokes can hold; there may be more truth, more emotional intensity, than the structures for communication can sustain.

Line 4 *'There is truth and confidence.*
Blood departs, fear goes away.
No mistake.'

The situation is genuinely frightening; you become indecisive, not sure whether what you're trying for is even possible. Here is the answer: be true, be confident. Confidence is an open channel that connects your small, daily work directly with creative inspiration. Such powerful motivation leaves no room for negativity or anxiety. Be more present, act with confidence, and the fear will go away by itself.

Line 5 *'There is truth and confidence as a bond.*
Rich in your neighbour.'

Truth and confidence creates strong, harmonious bonds between people. These are true riches.

Moreover, if there are things you want to achieve, or if you want to expand your capacity for growth, this can only be done through such bonds.

Line 6 *'Already rained, already come to rest.*
Honour the power it carries.
The wife's constancy brings danger,
The moon is almost full.
Noble one sets out to bring order – pitfall.'

Finally, those dense clouds have rained. You have received what you need for now; the energy is there for the crops to grow. Honour this, in all its wonderful, unknowable potential. The wife is defining and creating a home; the noble one is defining and creating a kingdom, with military expeditions to 'bring order' to its furthest regions. Yet there comes a point when their realm can't be made any safer, and the drive for more certainty becomes counterproductive.

The moon is almost full, the nights almost at their brightest, but the moon won't get any fuller than full. The rain has already come; you can't get it to rain for next year, too, just to make sure. The cycle turns, and all that remains to be cultivated now is patience and faith.

Hexagram 10, *Treading*

Key Questions

Where is the tiger?
Do you know how to work with such power?

Oracle

'Treading a tiger's tail.
It does not bite people.
Creating success.'

There are tigers in the outer world, and also inner tigers; as you get close, it's good to recognize the tiger for what it is.

Treading the tiger's tail is perilous – yet if you can move in harmony with it, you can invite its power into your own life as protection, fertility and blessing. To do this without getting bitten requires both skill and care.

Look to the power and intensity you are drawn to in the situation: its specific danger is there, and also its potential gift.

Image

'Heaven above, lake below: Treading.
A noble one differentiates above and below,
And makes a place for the people's aspiration.'

The depths of the sky are reflected in the lake as it dances below heaven. An awareness of other dimensions of reality enters inner dialogue, and this becomes aspiration: it's as natural for people to aspire as it is for the lake to reflect.

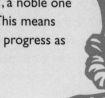

By marking out the difference between 'above and below', a noble one shows there is a direction to travel and a distance to cross. This means differentiating the ideal you aspire to from your step-by-step progress as you follow it.

Sequence

Treading follows from Hexagram 9, Small Taming:

'Things are tamed, and then there are the rituals. And so Treading follows.'

First you learn the rules for working with great power – inwardly or outwardly – and then you can move with it more freely and harmoniously.

CHANGING LINES

Line 1 *'Plain treading going on.*
        No mistake.'

What can you do when you realize you're not where you want to be? Simple: you move on, following your desire, lightly and responsively and without fuss.

There is no way to control everything or plan it all in advance – no need to wrestle with the tiger, just because it's there. You can only take one step at a time, so what is your simplest next step?

Line 2 *'Treading the path, smooth and easy.*
        A hermit's constancy brings good fortune.'

Hermits are hidden people, in retreat in the mountains. They walk their path with constancy, freedom and ease, because they are not concerned with anything other than their path. They don't take on responsibilities that are not their own; they are not influenced by negative relationships; they don't act out of the desire to have a particular effect or get a particular reaction from others. And so their path is naturally smooth and their treading is harmonious.

Line 3 *'With one eye, can see.*
        Lame, can walk.
        Treads on the tiger's tail:
        It bites him. Pitfall.
        Soldier acting as a great leader.'

When walking with tigers, 'making do' with capacities that are 'good enough' is not a good strategy. Here is someone who can see, but not the whole picture, and can move forward, but not in balance. This is like a soldier who lacks the capacity to lead, but who feels he must step up and take charge nonetheless. Bravery doesn't blunt the tiger's teeth.

Line 4 *'Treading the tiger's tail.*
Pleading, pleading.
Good fortune in the end.'

This is the moment when you are closest to the danger – and the moment when you can receive the tiger's gift. Tread extremely carefully, but be true: *ask for what you know you need.*

Such a path is lonely and dangerous: when you make your needs explicit, you become completely vulnerable. Yet this is the way to enter into a true relationship with the tiger, and so in the long run it will bring good fortune.

Line 5 *'Decisive treading.*
Constancy, danger.'

Your treading embodies who you are; what you choose declares your identity. When you decide to be fully present in everything you do, with nothing grudging or half-hearted, you make this *your* life.

Constancy on this path is dangerous: when you are highly individualistic, you may not fit in so well; people who are less sensitive to their surroundings, and to whatever isn't a part of their own identity, are not so easy to relate to.

Line 6 *'Observing the footsteps, blessings from the ancestors.*
They come full circle: good fortune from the source.'

Looking back over the tiger's path through your life (or perhaps it is your own path?) is like a form of divination, reading the footprints left by visiting animals. By looking at this 'track record', you open up to a larger communication, where you can perceive the shape and meaning of what has gone before. When you can see the footprints coming full circle – a completed pattern, and also the image of an endless cycle of communication – then their presence becomes a blessing.

Hexagram 11, *Flow*

Key Questions

How will you work with this extraordinary potential?
How can you channel the flow of energy to create harmony?

Oracle

'Flow. Small goes, great comes.
Good fortune, creating success.'

Flow is a sign of the free and full expression of tremendous creative energy. It is the name of China's most sacred mountain, *Tai*, which is imbued with spiritual power. The king would make great offerings at its summit to establish a flourishing, peaceful relationship with Heaven.

This is a time to create harmony with the greater flow, letting its energy pour into creative manifestation, as a river flows down into a fertile valley. Pettiness is swept away downstream, and the way opens for free communication. Great things become possible. The true scale of things is revealed, dwarfing your smaller concerns. You sense the powers that surge through your life, and know how far beyond your control they are – yet you can enter into true relationship with them and participate in Flow.

Image

'Heaven and Earth communicate: Flow.
The prince enriches and completes the way of heaven and earth,
Upholds and assists the order of heaven and earth,
To support and protect the people.'

Creative force flows through the earth; potential joins with the space for growth; everything is possible. The prince blessed with Flow wholly invests himself in bringing it to fruition in the human realm. He weaves the powers of inspiration and realization together into a synergistic context for creative work. To bring out its full potential, he will work actively to bring all people, energies and areas of life into harmony inside its embrace.

Sequence

Flow follows from Hexagram 10, Treading:

'Treading and also Flow, and then there is peace. And so Flow follows. Flow means flowing together.'

Treading behind the tiger, you learn to respond, dance and move skilfully with greater powers. With Flow, you come into close relationship with them. To be tranquil with such potent energy rather than engulfed by it, you will need to know how to Tread.

Pair

Flow is paired and contrasted with Hexagram 12, Blocked:

'Blocked and Flow are of opposite kind.'

In Flow, heaven and earth connect; in Blocked, they separate. Flow communicates; Blocked closes the channel. Flow makes everything possible; Blocked means nothing worthwhile can be achieved.

CHANGING LINES

Line 1   *'Pulling up thatch grass, roots entangled, with more of its kind.*
        Setting out to bring order, good fortune.'

If you try to pull up a single stem of thatch grass, you find it's connected to a dense, continuous web of roots below the surface. Here at the entry into Flow, acting on one point in the web can set it all in motion; sustained effort in small things will create synergy and momentum. This is an unusually powerful juncture: a single choice has more connections and consequences than you imagine. If you focus now on the harmony you want to experience, you can use this moment to start creating it, step by step.

Line 2   *'Embracing emptiness, use this to cross the river.*
        Not distancing yourself from what you leave behind,
        Friends disappear.
        Gaining honour, moving to the centre.'

There is nothing here for you. When you accept this emptiness, you find you are without any baggage or attachments at all, as if you were carrying only a hollow gourd. This will help you to cross the river swiftly

and lightly, single-mindedly committed to the transitions of your own journey.

You don't set out to distance yourself or cut anything out of your life; you only seek to participate in Flow. Yet as you move on, friends drop out of sight in a natural parting of the ways. You no longer belong; you're no longer recognized by a group of allies and peers. Instead, find honour and worth by going to the core of things: travel towards Mount Tai, the axis where creative spirit touches the world.

Line 3 *'There is no level ground without a slope,*
No going out without a return.
Constancy in hardship is no mistake.
Do not sorrow about its truth.
In eating and drinking there is blessing.'

Nothing is all smooth going; no journey is ever travelled in a straight line. Even when times are unusually hard, keep doing the work required each day to carry things through to completion. The hardship is not a drama or a catastrophe, it's just how things are – so why be unhappy with the only real world there is? Come gladly to the table and nourish yourself on the completeness of experience.

Line 4 *'Fluttering, fluttering.*
Not rich in your neighbours – not on guard against truth and confidence.'

You are like a bird out on the edge of the nest, feeling for the moment when wind and wings will hold you. You're filled with the desire to express your power freely and be yourself through action, but you hesitate on the point of take-off and don't quite commit yourself to the air. Your existing connections fail to provide the help and support you need – so rather than staying home and going on the defensive, you'll need to extend yourself and explore elsewhere. The truth is not a threat to you; nor is your own confidence.

Line 5 *'King Yi marries off his daughters.*
This brings fulfilment, good fortune from the source.'

Yi, a late Shang king, married his daughters into the Zhou clan, where their sons would found the Zhou dynasty. This represents a powerful choice to bring about union and harmony, in resonance with the joining of heaven and earth. It is a supremely auspicious moment, the source of great things. With patience, you can nourish the new creative potential and be confident it will reach fulfilment.

Line 6 *'The bulwarks fall back into the moat – don't use the army.*
From your own city, declaring the mandate.
Constancy means shame.'

The walls are in the moat, the city crumbles back to where it came from, and the ground is levelled again. There is no call for armies here: Flow has brought change, leaving nothing for them to attack or defend. The old constructions are simply no longer viable; there is no position to hold any more.

But at the summit of Mount Tai, a new ruler has come into harmony with the spirits and received the mandate from Heaven. Declare this mandate from your city: announce your authentic purpose from your own seat of authority. The soldiers can become farmers again, and cultivate new fields.

Hexagram 12, *Blocked*

Key Questions

What work can you do when nothing is working?
Who are you when no-one is noticing?

Oracle

'Blocking it, non-people.
Noble one's constancy bears no fruit.
Great goes, small comes.'

Nothing moves or grows, communication doesn't happen, everything is negated and blocked – and this is because of 'non-people'. That may mean that some people are a consistently, exclusively and pathologically negative influence and sabotage all attempts at progress. It can also refer to perceiving someone as not quite a real person, explaining their behaviour with labels and stereotypes rather than seeking to understand. In both cases, there is a complete failure of empathy.

This means that your very best and strongest efforts come to nothing. You can have a soaring imaginative concept of the creative possibilities here; you can have the will to be true to that concept and carry it through. You're not doing anything wrong; the problem is that these creative possibilities are just not available when things are Blocked. Small concerns dominate. The adaptive response is not to strive constantly to rise to a higher level, but to focus your attention on the small details – the immediate, uninspiring reality.

Image

'Heaven and earth do not interact: Blocked.
A noble one uses his strengths sparingly to avoid hardship.
He does not allow himself honours and payment.'

Inspiration soars upward; the opportunities for its realization sink ever further out of reach below. There is no creative connection between the two.

The noble one has noticed that the harder you bang your head against a brick wall, the more bruised you get, and so he is economical with his energy and talents. Equally, he does not look for rewards under this regime: the ones who are rewarded now are not noble. He has other priorities than external results and recognition.

Sequence

Blocked follows from Hexagram 11, Flow:

'Things cannot end with flowing together, and so Blocked follows.'

Effortless communication and mutual openness is a beautiful thing, but it cannot last forever – and perhaps it's somehow incomplete. Could it be that we need to be blocked and cut off so we can grow more strongly from deeper roots?

CHANGING LINES

Line 1 *'Pulling up thatch grass, roots entangled, with more of its kind.*
  Constancy, good fortune. Creating success.'

Thatch grass roots are tightly woven together, so you can't pull up one clump without finding yourself pulling up more and more. In a time of blockage, even questions that appear simple and manageable will turn out to be bound up with an endless tangle of issues.

 This makes the blockage harder to shift than you might have imagined. It would be futile to attempt to grasp the whole twisted mess of roots, to take on the whole situation at once. Yet if you pull on a single clump that fits within your grasp, and persist steadily and loyally, you will ultimately have an effect – if not necessarily the one you were looking for at first. The issues you face will be deeper and more far-reaching than you expected, but so too will the eventual benefits of your action.

Line 2 *'Embracing the charge.*
  Small people, good fortune.
  Great people, blocked. Creating success.'

You are offered an agreement like a contract, with its own set of mutual expectations, requirements and compensations. To embrace it is to accept the terms you are given, and enter into their service – something which has an utterly different significance for small and great people. (So if you contain both within yourself, they will be locked in a lively debate!)

 Small people don't expect to be in charge of their own destiny, and hence accept the role allotted to them. For them there is a gift concealed here – the chance to become part of something bigger than they could imagine on their own.

 Great people find the terms on offer – or the very idea of being 'under contract' – to be discordant with their values. What the small people find to be a blessing, they experience as a denial of what they are. So they challenge the limitations and refuse the agreement – and in so doing they see beyond its restricted scope to the full range of alternatives, and create success.

Line 3 *'Embracing shame.'*

You feel shame, and carry it enfolded within you, as part of yourself – whether or not you're fully aware of its influence. Since you don't feel entitled to anything much, you draw back into yourself and don't feel able to ask directly for what you want or need.

Line 4 *'There is a mandate, no mistake.*
Work with clarity, fulfilment.'

When you find yourself Blocked, it's hard to believe that your experience is meaningful. Nonetheless, there is a call to action in these events: a message you're meant to hear and work you're meant to be doing.

Having a mandate is unlikely to make your life easier; it tends to mean work. You watch for synchronicities and guidance; you take action on each insight; you cultivate yourself as a field to receive the signs and grow them to fulfilment. It takes sustained effort for the mandate to be fully realized – that, and adopting a clearer, broader perspective to allow patterns of meaning beyond your individual experience to come into view.

Line 5 *'Resting when blocked.*
Great person, good fortune.
It is lost, it is lost!
Tie it to the bushy mulberry tree.'

You are blocked; the 'openings' have all closed; there's nothing you can do. Rather than struggling on, take this as an opportunity to rest. The great person can use this breathing space to reflect and re-evaluate her course, to good effect.

It's easy to panic when you find you can't make a difference to your world through your actions – it creates a sense of vanishing opportunities, isolation and disconnection. But if you let go your attachment to everything that isn't working, and seek out the growing centre, you can regain a sense of the active possibilities in life. The mulberry tree, which regrows vigorously from its roots when cut back, promises life and new beginnings.

Line 6 *'Overturning the block.*
Before, blocked. Afterwards, rejoicing.'

Finally, the block can be overcome and the situation transformed so that negative forces become powerless. Gather yourself, make a concerted effort, and communication and flow will be restored.

Hexagram 13, *People in Harmony*

Key Questions

What are the unique contributions?
Where is the common ground?
How will your life change if your group expands?

Oracle

'People in harmony in the wilds: creating success.
Fruitful to cross the great river.
A noble one's constancy bears fruit.'

People create harmony with one another where they are of like mind and find common cause. They come out from the walls of their villages to forge alliances in the wild country – that is, they seek out common ground where they can meet, beyond the familiar boundaries that usually define the limits of 'people like us'. This means radically expanding the whole idea of who 'we' are.

Such fellowship is usually created between people – but it can also take place within an individual, for instance between inner selves, or between apparently unrelated traditions and ways of knowing. There is harmony when these are brought together in inner conversation to create strong alliances.

There is strength and energy in alliance. People in harmony can commit themselves further, take greater risks – they can cross the river and enter new territories. Once there is agreement, it's worthwhile to follow the vision tenaciously, with the constancy of a noble one.

Image

'Heaven joins with fire: People in Harmony.
A noble one sorts the clans and differentiates
between beings.'

Imagine the fire reaching up towards the night sky, joining with the stars to cast light on the many clans gathered around it. A noble one has the clarity of vision to see the shared nature all the groups have in common, and also what is shared only within each individual group, and how this distinctiveness comes from their clannish roots. Harmony between people will not come about by forcibly amalgamating the clans; to disarm their natural defensiveness, the noble one needs first to recognize and respect identities different from his own.

Sequence

People in Harmony follows from Hexagram 12, Blocked

'Things cannot end with blockage, and so People in Harmony follows.'

The exclusive, divisive mindset of 'us versus them' must be replaced by a larger sense of fellowship. Human awareness lights up the world, perceiving and creating the possibilities for co-creation and overcoming the drift apart of Hexagram 12.

Pair

People in Harmony forms a pair with Hexagram 14, Great Possession:

'Great possession means crowds, People in Harmony means connecting.'

There is power in groups and alliances – but the emphasis for now is on the human experience of harmony and connection, rather than on what might emerge.

CHANGING LINES

Line 1   *'People in harmony at the gate.*
          Not a mistake.'
Inside the walls is the familiar village; outside, a bigger world where more can be gained or lost. Those who think of venturing out naturally gather together here at the gate – a little band of potential fellow travellers, united by their willingness to explore. Their alliance is like a refuge from those who stay inside.

Gradually, you come to the gate and gather courage to brave the unknown. You may be concerned about what lies beyond the walls, but you're going in the right direction.

Line 2   *'People in harmony at the ancestral temple.*
          Shame.'

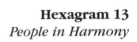

People find a sense of belonging and alliance at the ancestral temple – that is, at a place of deep shared roots and irreducible spiritual power.

But the temple cannot be used in this way. This is partly because, by failing to extend harmony beyond its walls, you are being too parochial in your thinking. The heady experience of unanimity within the temple may have blinded you to real differences beyond it.

And it is also because you are betraying the temple – those original principles and roots that you draw on – by using it just to feel secure. When you compare yourself with the purity of the ancestral ideal, it is fitting to feel shame. Those who come to the temple should surely bring an offering, not merely their needs.

Line 3 *'Hiding away arms in the thickets,*
Climbing your high mound.
For three years, not starting anything.'

In an atmosphere of suspicion and fear, the best you can do is to stow your resentment and your agenda well out of sight, and take the higher ground. With a strategic overview, it becomes clear that you cannot achieve anything here by winning a fight, but only by creating harmony. Since no one can be forced to share your agenda, disengage from inner or outer struggles and reconnect with your original intention.

Line 4 *'Bestriding your city walls,*
No one is capable of attack.
Good fortune.'

It's not easy to be in harmony with others if you feel constantly vulnerable. So the first step to peace is a robust boundary that protects the richness of your inner space. When you have this refuge that no one can possibly breach, there is no threat, and no need for any hostilities.

Line 5 *'People in harmony first cry out and weep, and then they laugh.*
Great leaders can bring them together.'

People come into harmony when they can see one another clearly. Only when everything is out in the light, all the feelings fully experienced and expressed, can they acknowledge one another. *Then* the tensions can be defused and the situation resolved. You will need fine leaders to make an alliance possible: on a personal level, that suggests tapping into your best self, the one who is genuinely in charge of your life.

Line 6 *'People in harmony at the outskirts altar.*
No regrets.'

Outside the walls, there is an altar-mound where many people can gather to make offerings. This is a wide open space, with enough room for everyone to be as they are without friction. And in the broadest, simplest sense possible, there is a shared interest that sets past conflicts in perspective. This doesn't mean that you can be in perfect agreement with everyone, but there is sufficient agreement that change can be accomplished. There will be no regrets for a phantom perfection; the past is left where it belongs, and a new phase begins.

Hexagram 14, *Great Possession*

Key Questions

Given all you have, who will you be?
How can you affirm and support what is good?

Oracle

'Great Possession.
From the source, creating success.'

Great Possession means you are rich – maybe in material goods, maybe in less tangible assets, like knowledge, wisdom, power, energy, talent or relationships. Whatever form it takes, you have something real and potent in your possession.

   The Chinese word for 'possession' also means 'there is', so this is 'great being' as well as 'great having': what there is and what you are, as well as what you have. The ancient form of the character shows an outstretched hand, which may hold an offering: to possess is to offer; what you have is, by definition, what you can give.

   And what you have and can give is great. This is pure potential: an opening to the source, and a promise of abundant energy ready to enter into circulation and become creatively active.

Image

'Fire dwells above heaven: Great Possession.
A noble one ends hatred and spreads the good,
She yields to heaven and rests in her mandate.'

The stars move in their courses in accordance with natural law. A noble one has an inner awareness of creative reality, and carries this through into insight and clarity in living. The greatness of the cosmos is that it works as it should, and so her task is quite simple: to allow it to be, remove obstacles, and work with it.

   Hatred would only waste energy resisting reality; spreading the good aligns with the natural order. The sun does not struggle to rise in the sky, it just rises; in the same way, because a noble one assents to what is and yields to heaven, she can rest in her work.

Sequence

Great Possession follows from Hexagram 13, People in Harmony:

'Reaching out to people in harmony means beings truly return home, and so Great Possession follows.'

With harmony, beings come into their right places, true relationships form, and a flow of exchange – of having and giving – is set in motion. Exchange *is* wealth, and so Great Possession follows: the emergent power of relationship, always greater than the sum of its parts.

CHANGING LINES

Line 1 *'No interaction with what is harmful,
In no way at fault,
So that hardship is not a mistake.'*

You are involved in an ongoing act of creation, selecting the ingredients of Great Possession. Whatever you introduce now, you will possess in great measure later on. So pay careful attention to the contents of your thoughts and your relationships with others; don't engage or connect in any way with anything that would do harm.

If (and only if) you find you can be a purely, consistently constructive force, then it is not a mistake to take on challenges and work your way through hardship: you'll be sustained by the knowledge that you are still on the right path.

Line 2 *'A great chariot to carry loads.
With a direction to go, no mistake.'*

A great chariot is big enough to move great possessions – carrying you, and your life, to a new place. This should be used to move on; the only mistake would be to stay in the same place, imagining that you're stuck.

Clarify where you are, and what you have, and how this enables you to travel onward. Hold a vision in mind of where you want to arrive, and set out to explore.

Line 3 *'A prince makes a summer offering to the son of heaven.
Small people are in no way capable of this.'*

A prince has visionary qualities: he understands that great possession means more than just 'having', and he can see beyond what there is to what is possible. He has confidence in the real value of his work and wealth, and so he is glad to dedicate it to something higher.

But small people are too preoccupied with the business of survival for such visions; they cannot afford to spend their scarce resources unless they are sure of immediate returns. And in any case, they may not believe that what they have is of sufficient value to be offered.

Which of these are you, and which will you be?

Line 4 *'It is not for you to dominate,*
No mistake.'

It is not for you to dominate the situation. Trying to get everyone and everything to march to the loud beat of your drum is not necessary, and the attempt would most likely be counterproductive. Both you and the situation will be fine even when you are not in control.

Naturally you want your gifts to be fully expressed and used – but it could be more productive in the long run to master those gifts, so you can apply them more discriminately, in a way that fits the situation and communicates well with others. This allows you to grow into a personal strength which has very little to do with being dominant.

Line 5 *'Your truth interacts, strikes awe –*
Good fortune.'

Pure, undiminished truth communicates directly and with great force. It is not compromised by trying to convey a specific message or create a particular outcome, but speaks consistently and powerfully through what it is.

You will make the most profound and lasting difference simply by being who you are, without dilution and without ulterior motives.

Line 6 *'From heaven comes help and protection.*
Good fortune,
Nothing that does not bear fruit.'

Everything is unfolding in accordance with the way of the cosmos. Whether or not this is the way you had in mind, it is good fortune; it will bear fruit, though perhaps not as you anticipated. You can participate in the energy of this natural order; there's no need to force things to happen in a certain way.

Hexagram 15, *Integrity*

Key Questions

What is the simple reality?
How might you return to a state of balance?
What if it didn't all depend on you?

Oracle

*'Integrity creates success.
A noble one completes it.'*

To experience Integrity is like coming face to face with your real self – plain, simple and unadorned. To have Integrity is to be whole, at one with yourself and with reality. It means being honest about your own capacities, holding yourself in creative balance with your world and not exaggerating the importance of your role.

These qualities enable the noble one to bring whatever work presents itself to completion. Since she is not overly full of herself, she has space for the real world; she isn't hampered by an excess or by a lack of confidence. Since she isn't caught up in a personal story, and doesn't identify her work with her worth, she is free to do what needs to be done and move on.

Image

*'In the centre of the earth there is a mountain: Integrity.
A noble one reduces what is too much and increases what is diminished.
Weighing things up to even out their distribution.'*

The earth is unassuming and supports all beings; you might never realize that it contains the height and solidity of a mountain at its centre. A noble one is inwardly as self-sufficient as a mountain and as firm as bedrock; she has quietly built up the inner resources to sustain an intelligent, centred generosity. She reduces exaggeration and brings things back to a state of equilibrium, weighing up what is needed from moment to moment, and always referring back to that inner balance point.

Sequence

Integrity follows from Hexagram 14, Great Possession:

'Great possession means being incapable of arrogance, and so Integrity follows.'

Integrity does not mean a false humility. When we are confident in our gifts, we can see ourselves in true proportion with everything and everyone else, and we become capable of integrity.

Pair

Integrity forms a pair with Hexagram 16, Enthusiasm:

'Integrity takes itself lightly; Enthusiasm is careless.'

Integrity is simple and down to earth; Enthusiasm is grand and adventurous, enlarging your sense of self through colourful images and stories. Neither is very concerned about outcomes, but for different reasons: Enthusiasm might insist that nothing can go wrong for you, while Integrity suggests that what happens to you isn't such an important matter.

CHANGING LINES

Line 1 *'At one in integrity, the noble one*
Uses this to cross the great river.
Good fortune.'

The noble one pays attention and holds firmly to what is real, and her integrity moves her to act. It lends her the courage to take risks and commit herself: it's easier to cross rivers when you are not weighed down by a demanding self-image. She will cross into new territory without asking for guarantees, reliant only on herself.

   When you honestly perceive a need to act, it is important to get underway, discovering and creating new possibilities without a great burden of expectations. Achievement has little to do with being recognized, and everything to do with venturing out and exploring.

Line 2 *'The call of integrity.*
Constancy, good fortune.'

This means giving voice to your unique inner nature, speaking out with honesty that is not compromised by trying to elicit a certain response. The call is not a demand, or evangelism, but simply the sound of your authentic presence. When you live in accord with this over time, moving forward steadily and consistently, it brings good fortune.

Line 3 *'Toiling with integrity,*
A noble one completes it.
Good fortune.'

You have demanding work to do, but with the qualities of the noble one you can complete it. Others may not see why you are doing this; they may not know of your work at all. But the important thing is not that it's seen to be done, only that it gets done. You are lending all your strength to a greater, longer-term goal; seeing your task in that context will strengthen your inner determination.

Line 4 *'Nothing that does not bear fruit,*
Displaying integrity.'

When you have integrity, you are at one with yourself and your world; every encounter, every detail, is a chance to respond authentically, and so everything in your experience bears fruit. Then you can communicate with no need for grand gestures or carefully-designed messages: even your smallest actions are always sending a clear signal, without interference.

Line 5 *'Not rich in your neighbour,*
Fruitful to use this to invade and conquer.
Nothing that does not bear fruit.'

When times are hard, you look for help first to what is nearby – your current circumstances and nearest relationships. If you don't find what you need here, you have a choice. You could settle politely for what you have: there might be enough for subsistence, though not for you to flourish. Or you could use its inadequacies as an inspiration to venture further afield and conquer something new. Seeking fulfilment – a higher and larger goal than just getting by – is the path of integrity; it is hard, challenging work, but it bears fruit.

Line 6 *'The call of integrity.*
Fruitful to use this to mobilize the army,
And bring order to city and state.'

Who you are sings out. When you listen to this call, you can use its energy to galvanize all your resources, reclaiming the initiative to bring about change. You clear out inauthenticity, overcome unrest and create harmony – acting with calm and clear intention, and always only within your own realm of responsibility. This brings your life into resonance with your true voice, so your full potential can find expression.

Hexagram 16, *Enthusiasm*

Key Questions

What do you imagine?
What inspires you?
How can you use your enthusiasm constructively?

Oracle

'Enthusiasm.
Fruitful to set up feudal lords and mobilize the armies.'

The Chinese word for 'enthusiasm' contains an elephant – a character that also means 'image'. The elephant is magnificent, strong, a source of delight – and also unpredictable and potentially dangerous. Imagination and anticipation move us with ease; with them, we can be motivated and inspired – or we can be carried away by the power of our own story.

The energetic charge of enthusiasm can be used to set great things in motion. It is good to use it to expand and enrich your experience by extending your network of communication and support, marshalling your resources ready for future challenges. And it is also good to use such structures to channel the motive power of enthusiasm, and keep it from running amok. Then its brightly coloured images can be woven securely into the larger patterns and meanings of life.

Image

'Thunder bursts forth from the earth: Enthusiasm.
The ancient kings composed music to honour virtue,
They celebrated and worshipped the supreme lord,
Joining with their ancestors.'

Thunder bursts forth from the quiet earth in spring, waking the plants, stirring everything into growth. The ancient kings channelled the joy of spring into music: singing with the thunder, the people participate in ever rising energies. Their spontaneous emotion becomes part of a rich and subtle fabric of relationships – the harmony of music, veneration for the supreme divinity, and the family of the ancestors.

Sequence

Enthusiasm follows from Hexagram 15, Integrity:

'One who possesses greatness and is also capable of Integrity is naturally Enthusiastic.'

Integrity grounds Enthusiasm, giving its potent images the foundation in ordinary reality that makes them visions rather than fantasies. Someone who has an authentic vision of great potential cannot help but be enthusiastic.

CHANGING LINES

Line 1 *'Enthusiasm calling out,*
Pitfall.'

This does not begin on firm ground: enthusiasm's call may arise from a sense of insecurity, looking to be guided or supported. It is triggered by circumstances, and made impulsively, without much awareness of or reflection on its purpose. Enthusiasm sings its own song, and does not harmonize with anyone or anything else. The results are never good.

Line 2 *'Boundaries turning to stone,*
Not for a whole day.
Constancy, good fortune.'

Boundaries are meant to provide structure and defence, armouring you against negative influences and asserting control. And for a time they offer rock-solid protection.

But boundaries work best when they are porous, allowing exchange and communication, and these boundaries are turning into a trap. They cannot last much longer, not even to the end of the day: the will to communicate, move and change is stronger than rock, and your purpose is more durable than your boundaries. Let them crumble, stay constant to the vision that motivates you, and there will be good fortune.

Line 3 *'Enthusiasm gazing upward, regret.*
Procrastination brings regret.'

You look outward, always watching for your cue, waiting for someone else to make a move, or for the exact right time to act. But what you are looking for out there never comes, and nor does the perfect moment – and meanwhile, you have altogether missed the *present* moment, where you might have found your natural response and initiative. So you lose touch with your motivation, and delay a little longer – and end up regretting lost opportunities and unfulfilled potential.

Line 4 *'Source of enthusiasm.*
Great possessions gained.
Do not doubt.
Partners are gathered together as a hair clasp gathers hair.'

You have the initiative: your own inner motivation and enthusiasm can become a magnetic, creative force and bring you what you seek. Even if it's hard to imagine how success could be possible, there's no need to doubt yourself: the very fact that you imagine the possibility gives it the space and energy to grow. Your willingness is at the centre, both gathering your own strengths and resources, and also inspiring a response in others.

Line 5 *'Constancy, sickness.*
Persevering, not dying.'

Holding steady to your chosen path takes you through anxiety and sickness. The struggle and distress clarify the image of what you want to create, and you see it as part of an important whole. So you persevere doggedly in trying to make this image real, in the hope that real life will tell the story you want it to – and you do keep it from dying, though it never quite comes to life.

Line 6 *'Enthusiasm in the dark.*
Results bring a change of heart,
No mistake.'

You are full of imaginings, intensely emotionally involved, but utterly lacking in clarity. Perhaps you are being unrealistic – or perhaps you already know that you are feeling your way in the dark, with no clear sense of what is really out there, or really possible. Once you get some tangible results, then you can begin to perceive things in their right proportions. If your imaginings can be grounded in reality, you no longer need to worry about nursing false enthusiasm.

Hexagram 17, *Following*

Key Questions

How are things flowing, and how can you move with them?
Where are you being nudged and guided?

Oracle

'Following.
From the source, creating success, constancy bears fruit.
No mistake.'

Energy flows strongly into life's landscapes, bringing a great creative drive, from the source
through towards fulfilment. Following it means a willingness to honour the flow and align actions
with it. You can know your ideal, and then allow it to meld with the natural current, following
signs and nudges and allowing them to draw you onward.

Then, you may experience Following as an effortless flow of supportive synchronicities – or
you may experience it as events unfolding in accordance with their own schedule, and failing to
keep to yours. It can seem as if simply allowing yourself to be guided by the current is not
enough, and you ought to be 'doing something'. But moving with the creative process is not a
mistake.

Image

'At the centre of the lake is thunder: Following.
A noble one at nightfall
Goes inside for renewal and rest.'

In spring, the dragon flies out over the fields and brings rain,
but over winter he sleeps at the bottom of the lake. As
the dragon and the noble one know, energy is stored up
below the level of conscious activity, and so to connect
with it you need to go inside and sleep. Instead of
obsessively pursuing your desires, stop and rest in
accordance with the season.

Sequence

Following comes from Hexagram 16, Enthusiasm:

'Enthusiasm naturally means Following.'

When you have a great vision, things and people are naturally carried along by it. And it could be that what first visited you as inspiration corresponds with a larger, more fundamental energy, that you experience now as an inner momentum to events.

Pair

Following is paired and contrasted with Hexagram 18, Corruption.

'Following has no causes. Corruption, and then order.'

Following, you live in the present. Events are not experienced as the effects of causes; they arise spontaneously in the moment. But Corruption marks a time for investigating the causes of negative effects, setting life on a more solid foundation.

CHANGING LINES

Line 1 *'An official has a change of heart.*
Constancy, good fortune.
Going out of the gates, joining with others, there is achievement.'
To begin following, first step outside your official role, so you have more allegiance to your fellow humans, and to truth, and less to formalities and positions. It's good to carry this right through, so that you leave your familiar corner behind and go all the way out of the gates, where you can participate in the whole group and be guided by its larger story.

Line 2 *'Bound to the small child,*
Letting the mature man go.'
The child is still unformed and open to all possible futures; he is more guided by interaction with others than by a personal sense of direction. He is light and spontaneous, not settled and responsible. You're tending to bind yourself to the small child; if you do so, you lose the mature man. This can be an inner or outer bond – to a person or a role and way of being. In either case, it's a very simple alternative: you cannot be, or have, both.

Line 3 *'Bound to the mature man,*
Letting the small child go.
Following, there is quest and gain.
Settling with constancy bears fruit.'

There is a choice between the mature man and the small child, as a way of being or as an association to follow. To choose the adult is to take responsibility for creating change, and lose the open, carefree nature of the child. The adult makes his choice and pursues it with an earnest steadiness of purpose; then, hopefully, he stops and makes himself at home with what he has attained.

Line 4 *'Following makes a catch. Constancy, pitfall.*
With truth and confidence, holding to the path with clarity,
How can this be wrong?'

There's a fine line between following an ideal, and becoming so intent on your goals that you lose touch with immediate reality – especially if your goal is to receive some particular response you've come to depend on. It's the difference between holding confidently to what is here – the present moment, your path and its direction – and clutching for a false security. Being in motion, on your path, allowing yourself to be guided, is never a mistake.

Line 5 *'True and confident in excellence.*
Good fortune.'

As you move with change, ask yourself what you value most highly, and hold to that through all the upheaval. Good fortune comes of being true to your achievements and confident in your path's unfolding.

Line 6 *'Seized and bound to it,*
And so joining and connected to it,
The king makes offering on the Western mountain.'

The king on the Western mountain has gone to the very source of the energy that flows into life. By making offering here, he identifies his will with the flow. This is like seizing and binding, and also like close relationship and alliance – a time of dedication and of firm bonds between people.

   You can be free and spontaneous and still tightly bound; you can lead when matters are out of your hands.

Hexagram 18, *Corruption*

Key Questions

What is behind this trouble?
What is the hidden cause?

Oracle

'Corruption. Creating success from the source.
Fruitful to cross the great river.
Before the seed day, three days. After the seed day, three days.'

In ancient China, ancestors angered by neglect would send sickness and misfortune. This is corruption: something dark, like a curse, lurking under the surface of life and manifesting as patterns of negative experience. We don't have to believe in angry ancestors to be haunted by corruption, whether we inherit its darkness from our past, our culture, or through our parents.

When you receive Hexagram 18, it is time to examine those old, old patterns at last, to seek out their source and give it due honour and attention. When you understand where your experience comes from, you can restore the creative flow and make a genuinely new beginning.

You will need to commit yourself to the journey and take the risk of crossing the great river into unknown territory. And you will need to pay careful attention to the process. Before 'seed day', which marks the beginning of a new cycle of time, you'll need to identify the source of the corruption and prepare for change. Afterwards, you need to pay attention to the needs of the new growth. Each of these phases has only a modest duration; you're invited to attend and examine, but not to dwell on this change for a lifetime.

Image

'Below the mountain is the wind: Corruption.
A noble one rouses the people to nurture character.'

The mountain traps and limits the movement of the wind, making for stale, unhealthy air – an invisible corruption, poisoning from within. But a noble one transforms this picture: he stirs people up like the wind, and nurtures their character like a sheltering mountain. This can work among people or within an individual: inner movement and awakening transform limitation into a protective covering for growth.

Sequence

Corruption follows from Hexagram 17, Following.

'Following people with joy means there are things to be done, and so Corruption follows. Corruption means things to be done.'

Following is simply guided from moment to moment by the invisible currents beneath the surface of events. Eventually, the flow carries you to a place where 'there are things to be done', and it's time to interrogate the hidden causes and bring them into the light of day.

CHANGING LINES

Line 1 *'Ancestral father's corruption.*
There is a child,
The deceased elders are without fault.
Danger. In the end, good fortune.'

The first step into engaging with corruption is to choose and own it as your inheritance. The child steps forward to take responsibility, and the forefathers are without fault; you no longer blame your parents or your past for whatever has gone wrong. It is dangerous to engage so closely and personally with the angry old ghosts, but there is no other way to empower yourself to begin this work, which will bring about good fortune in the end.

Line 2 *'Ancestral mother's corruption,*
Does not allow constancy.'

The mother is profoundly committed to provide nourishment and space for her family to grow. The ancestral mother's corruption means that this provision and commitment isn't working: it is not possible to carry this situation through to the desired outcome. What's started is not sustainable; things cannot come to full growth.

Perhaps a lack of resources means there is not enough available to give. Perhaps the reality of the situation simply makes your vision unfeasible, and 'mother's corruption' lies in not letting go. In any case, you cannot bring about the resolution you want just by forging on.

Instead, you need to develop personal boundaries, neither too rigid nor too porous, that allow you to respond without reacting. You need to recapture some independence of soul.

Line 3 *'Ancestral father's corruption.*
There is small regret,
No great mistake.'

You want to deal with corruption and move on, setting life on a firmer footing. To do so, though, you need a response – from an individual, or from the cosmos at large – so you know where you are and have something more solid to build on.

Such responses are not simply available for the asking. You need to be very persistent and clear in your request, and this can easily tip over into being pushy and anxious and going too far. So there is small regret – perhaps you could have managed this better, or more calmly – but no great mistake. Your basic desire to understand and move forward is not wrong at all.

Line 4 *'Comfortable with the father's corruption.*
Going on sees shame.'

The situation is fundamentally corrupt. Only a thoroughgoing reform of the whole structure will create a healthy environment for future growth.

However, you're reluctant to take on responsibility for such a decisive change. You don't want to see how rotten things have become; you find you can tolerate the situation, and live in the expectation – or just the hope – that it will all sort itself out somehow.

But in fact the real situation is not sustainable, and if you go on this will become painfully apparent.

Line 5 *'Ancestral father's corruption.*
Use praise.'

You can deal with what's wrong by concentrating on what's right, when tackling the problem directly might provoke resistance. With praise, or any kind of intervention that speaks to what is alive and healthy, you are gently bypassing the corruption altogether to reach the growing seed: the inner idealist, with a child's vision of possibilities.

Line 6 *'No business with kings and lords,*
Honouring what is highest is your business.'

It's true that we need to deal with corruption, and establish a healthy relationship with inner or outer authority figures. But this is not an end in itself. There comes a time when that work is done, and all that's left is empty politics. This is not your concern: it's time to leave it behind, rejoin the larger world and honour a higher aspiration. It may be harder to see, but it is more real.

Hexagram 19, *Nearing*

Key Questions

How does this want to grow?
How can you take responsibility for its development?
What would your greater self do?

Oracle

'Nearing.
Creating success from the source, constancy bears fruit.
Reaching an end in the eighth month means a pitfall.'

'Nearing' means drawing closer and gazing down over what you approach. There are two strands of meaning here: the approach of a greater spirit or presence in an ongoing process of growth, and your approach as the one who pays attention and takes responsibility.

Like the creative drive of Hexagram 1, this great, growing energy comes from the source, asks for your full participation, and seeks to reach fruition and be realized. But its surging growth can be disastrously interrupted by 'reaching an end in the eighth month'.

The eighth month is the month of harvest. If this comes round too soon for what Nears to reach full growth – if the situation demands that you produce a tangible result prematurely – then this means misfortune. Or if you focus exclusively on results instead of watching patiently over developments – if your expectations are out of touch with the pace of growth – then there is misfortune.

Having something to show for a process of growth doesn't mean you've arrived at its outcome: harvest is not the end. As each harvest is gathered in and stored, the seasonal cycle of growth continues; you need to stay present to its ongoing changes, wherever they might lead.

Image

'Above the lake is earth: Nearing.
A noble one teaches and reflects untiringly,
Accepts and protects the people without limit.'

A noble one has the inner reflective depths of the lake, contained within the protective, accepting qualities of the earth. She is the one with endless capacity to reflect, interact and explain, to shelter and nurture people as a parent protects a child. She has the strength and maturity, and so naturally she becomes responsible.

Sequence

Nearing follows from Hexagram 18, Corruption:

'With work to do, greatness becomes possible, and so Nearing follows. Nearing means greatness.'

The experience of dealing with Corruption gives rise to Nearing. What was once a curse becomes a source of strength; by doing the work of dealing with the old poisons, you create a secure foundation for your greater self to emerge. No negative pattern or insecurity need remain to obstruct the processes of growth.

Pair

Nearing forms a pair with Hexagram 20, Seeing:

'What is right for Nearing and Seeing: someone reaches out, someone seeks.'

Hexagrams 19 and 20 respond to one another: Seeing watches for Nearing to approach and reach out. They connect, and each completes the other. When you are Nearing, you become the help, guidance or opportunity waiting to be Seen.

CHANGING LINES

Line 1 *'Influence nearing.*
Constancy, good fortune.'
Nearing is felt first of all as an influence — an inkling of connection and presence, a moving spirit that opens you up and draws you into relationship. When such beginnings inspire constancy, this leads to good fortune: when you sense the emergent potential, you can be moved to take on responsibility to foster and guide its growth. That doesn't mean creating rules for their own sake, but only a certain order and coherence so that the influence can be more clearly felt. The greater your inner focus

and concentration, the more present and available you can become.

Line 2 *'Influence nearing, good fortune.*
Nothing that does not bear fruit.'

Nearing is felt as an inner influence and connection: a return of energy, perhaps as if you were reawakening and coming back to yourself. When you see this as part of a greater whole, everything about it is good and fruitful – even the parts that slip from your control, or hurt, or don't go according to plan.

Line 3 *'Sweetness nearing,*
No direction bears fruit.
Already grieving it, no mistake.'

The experience or the person drawing near promises to be exclusively sweet, amenable and nice. This is not just too good to be true, it's too one-sided to be whole or real. No amount of planning or intending can somehow turn pure sweetness into complete nourishment and make this sustainable. You are not wrong to grieve this and let it go.

Line 4 *'An end nearing,*
No mistake.'

The Oracle for this hexagram says that reaching an end in the eighth month means a pitfall. Now, there almost is an end; you are arriving. Completion is in sight, and with it personal fulfilment. Have patience and confidence; if you haven't arrived yet, it's because it's not yet time to arrive. So long as your intuitive, natural self is in charge, everything will unfold as it should.

Line 5 *'Realization nearing.*
Right for a great leader.
Good fortune.'

Now understanding and insight are nearing. Such realization is what you need to act as a great leader, one who has the measure of the situation and trusts her own awareness. The presence of insight enables you to create a harmonious, working alliance between emotion and reality. Then your decisions bring good fortune.

Line 6 *'Great-hearted nearing*
Good fortune, no mistake.'

This is generous, genuine nearing: it honours the one it nears, and has no ulterior motives. To draw near in this way might mean letting go of your own desires for a particular outcome right now – understanding that the ongoing process of growth is more important than anything you get along the way.

Hexagram 20, *Seeing*

Key Questions

When you stop searching, what comes into view?
If you had no preconceptions, what might you see?

Oracle

'Seeing. Washing hands, and not making the offering.
There is truth and confidence like a presence.'

To see is not to focus on some specific thing, but to witness everything that comes into view, with open awareness like a heron seeing a lake.

In the ritual, the everyday world is washed off — and then there is a breathless pause. It is not yet time to make the offering, but only to watch for what comes, 'like a presence', into the space.

In ordinary life, also, you can pause before falling automatically into the next step of the process, and see what is present before you respond. Into this space between actions comes truth, its presence as unmistakable as a great person's aura. You need only watch for it as it comes.

Image

'Wind moves over the earth: Seeing.
The ancient kings studied the regions,
Saw the people,
And established their teachings.'

The wind blowing over the earth follows its contours, and so it moves freely and goes everywhere. The influence of the wise kings travelled just as freely because they understood that to convey any idea, share any plan or impart any wisdom, it works best to be as fluid as the wind. They did not set out to impose a predetermined, rigid curriculum regardless of lived reality; that would have left people unable to relate to the teachings. They went out first to See real people and study the nuances of their daily lives; *then* they could teach.

Sequence

Seeing follows from Hexagram 19, Nearing:

'What is great allows Seeing.'

The presence that Nears in Hexagram 19 has greatness: when you embody this, you can be truly present to what is, without needing it to be something else – and then you can See.

Also, what is great can be Seen: those who witness the space between actions realize that 'there is truth and confidence like a presence'. Unrestricted Seeing provides a quality of attention that naturally draws out greatness.

CHANGING LINES

Line 1 *'A child seeing.*
For small people, no mistake.
For a noble one, shame.'

A child sees the world without being able to change anything about it. She depends on others, and so naturally she has the perspective of a dependant, imagining the whole world in the only way that makes sense to her: 'What will it mean for me? What will I get?'

If you are a small person, someone who can only adapt and be flexible, then this is your way: small people must watch the workings of power and try to anticipate its impact on their own lives. If you are a noble one, you might start out with a child's perspective, but you would be ashamed not to grow beyond it.

Line 2 *'Peeping through, seeing.*
A woman's constancy is fruitful.'

This is peeping through a narrow space, like someone who looks out through the crack of the door to see what's coming, but without showing or committing herself. You don't interact directly with the world outside, and you're not in a strong position to influence it, but you have the opportunity simply to see what is there – if only with a restricted angle of view.

When your seeing is restricted, it's natural to concentrate on looking for what will be of most help to you: after all, you don't need to understand the whole picture just now. Nonetheless, it's good to remember that you are only catching a glimpse of a completely new scene, far more expansive than the narrow slice that's immediately visible to you, and to stay open to those broader possibilities. This is a woman's constancy: committing not just to realize a known goal, but to receive and nurture a potential for growth, and responding fluidly in each moment to provide what it needs.

Line 3 *'Seeing my life.*
Advancing, withdrawing.'

Now you can let your whole life come into view, and start to see what you are creating. It's a moment of transition, and it can feel very strained, as if you were pulling in two directions at once. You advance, become more involved, enter into things; you withdraw and pull back; you do each in turn, or both at once. The oracle does not say that one direction is better than the other. Instead of experiencing this as a conflict, try seeing the to-and-fro pattern you create, like the steps in a dance of engagement.

Line 4 *'Seeing the realm shining out.*
Fruitful and useful to be a guest of the king.'

You are naturally drawn towards a shining realm: its light calls to you, promising that there is something for you here – work, gifts, insight. By entering into this realm modestly, like a guest, you enjoy the full benefit of its energy; you may start to see beyond its radiance and understand what it has to offer you. And also, you can stop here: you can pause and see the realm, without identifying with it, or imagining that you own it, or it owns you.

Line 5 *'Seeing my own life.*
The noble one is without mistake.'

The fifth line is traditionally the place for the ruler, and there is a Chinese understanding that the ruler has ultimate moral and spiritual responsibility for everything that happens in his kingdom. You are invited to see your life as the king sees his realm, as something you are creating, with all its elements coming together to form a complete image of who you are.

This is not an easy thing to see: it strips away whatever other self-image you might have developed, maybe clearing out some preconceptions or plans along with it. When the noble one can step into this newly cleared space, to see and own his own life without delusions of grandeur or guilt, he will be able to act without mistake.

Line 6 *'Seeing their lives.*
The noble one is without mistake.'

The ruler at the fifth line saw how his whole life was about him. Here at the sixth line, a sage looks out from the mountain top and sees how nothing in the world is about him. He can watch over the whole pattern of relationships, choices and affinities from here, and not take any of it personally. When the noble one sees this bird's eye view, needs nothing from it and yet remains committed, he will be able to act without mistake.

Hexagram 21, *Biting Through*

Key Questions

What must you do to get to the truth?
How can you become more effective?

Oracle

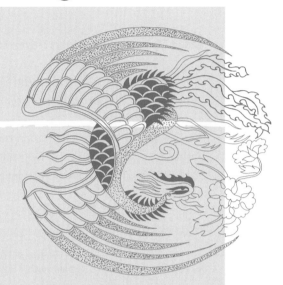

*'Biting through, creating success.
Fruitful to use legal proceedings.'*

It's time to bite through to the truth, cracking the situation open like a bone between your teeth, using the power of a diviner to open up the smooth surfaces of things and penetrate to the essence. Resting content with appearances may be easier, but it is no longer enough.

Deal with obstacles as you would something tough in your food: bite and gnaw your way through until your teeth meet. It will help to use the determination of an investigator or a judge, intent on restoring the world to good order, who will let nothing stand between them and the truth.

Image

*'Thunder and lightning: Biting Through.
The ancient kings brought light to punishments and enforced the laws.'*

Thunder and lightning come together, like action and insight. The ancient kings, who had the task of keeping the world in good order, understood that punishment and enforcement alone were not enough: there had to be light. We need to see and understand the laws of life in order to have insight into the connection between what we do and what happens to us. Punishing experience comes like a bolt of lightning that jolts us into recognizing how we live in relationship to those laws. When you can feel pain, you know that you are awake and your circulation is flowing.

Sequence

Biting Through follows from Hexagram 20, Seeing:

'Capable of seeing, hence there is a place for uniting, and so Biting Through follows. Biting Through means uniting.'

Once you allow everything to come into view, you can be sure of grasping the whole situation, rather than focusing too narrowly and failing to see the real obstacle. So when you can See, you have the possibility of reaching a specific truth, or a particular result.

Pair

Biting Through forms a pair with Hexagram 22, Beauty:

'Biting Through means eating; Beauty is without colour.'

There's a time for reaching the truth, and a time for expressing it. Biting through, you take the situation into yourself, 'chew it over' and digest it; Beauty will bring out its pure, plain essence.

CHANGING LINES

Line 1 *'Shoes locked in the stocks, feet disappear - not a mistake.'*
Locked in the stocks, you are not free to move, explore or communicate spontaneously. You can't act on your ideas, because someone or something stronger than you has other plans.

Yet the constraint that keeps you stuck here doesn't need biting through: the situation is not a mistake, and there is nothing to be gained by allocating blame. The stocks frustrate you, but you are safe: you can't run into trouble. Instead of following your plans any further into a world of unforeseen complications, you have time to reflect and concentrate on what is within your scope. Since there's no need for you to be anywhere else just yet, this is your chance to find a simpler, more effective approach.

Line 2 *'Biting into meat so your nose disappears - not a mistake.'*
A new, different flavour of food is available – something outside your usual realm of experience. Instead of sniffing at what you're offered cautiously to compare it with what you know, or decide whether this is wholesome, or even whether it's what you were looking for, you simply get stuck in. And you do so with such sheer appetite that you lose the use of your sense of smell, of discrimination, altogether. This may seem incautious, trusting too much and planning too little. However, freely immersing yourself in the full

experience – without formality, demands or expectations – is certainly a very direct, immediate way to gain insight into its nature and whether or not it is nourishing for you.

Line 3 *'Biting into dried meat, coming on poison.*
Small shame, not a mistake.'

What you're biting on here is tough, but you keep going – hoping for nourishment, connection or insight. Just gnawing on through will not be enough, though: there is poison hidden away in the meat. This is not edible, much less nourishing; things will not work as you'd hoped, so you must change your plans.

This is no public humiliation, but you still feel a small, personal shame that you have got so far off track – compounded by the fact that even when you see what's wrong, you still lack the means to set it right. But this is no time to sink into depression: now you realize that this meat is bad, you have the insight and understanding you need to go in search of better food.

Line 4 *'Biting into dried, bony meat, gains a metal arrow.*
Constancy in hardship bears fruit – good fortune.'

Dried, bony meat is tough and contains no worthwhile nourishment. Even enormously hard work will never yield the rewards you seek. You might be tempted to give up – but if you let yourself be deterred, you would never discover the shining metal arrowhead, hidden in the meat.

This arrow is still not what you were hoping for: it's a different kind of reward, valuable on a completely new level. This is not perishable flesh, but fine, enduring metal, heavy and solid in your hand. It does not feed you; it gives you the means to catch better food independently. Like the intense focus and determination that kept you persevering, it will always fly straight and true. Through single-minded persistence, you gain skills, resourcefulness and a concentrated inner strength.

Line 5 *'Biting through dried meat, gaining golden metal.*
Constancy means danger – not a mistake.'

You are engaging with tough, longstanding problems, and this is hard work. By persisting, and not allowing present or possible future difficulties to frighten you away, you can find gold: something pure, true and imperishable. There is an authentic reason why you are involved here, a shining promise, and this holds its value no matter what happens.

There's a risk that your determination could become an anxious struggle for security, caught up in fear of loss and a need to control people and outcomes – which you can't do. Deliberately biting into such tough meat might seem to be inviting the risk of injury. Yet the issues can't be avoided indefinitely – and when you do your own part (and only your own part) in tackling them, there is gold to be found.

Line 6 *'Shouldering a cangue so your ears disappear – pitfall.'*

A cangue is a punishment device, like wooden stocks carried round the neck, and this one is so big and heavy that it covers your ears. Here is someone who cannot hear the truth: it's not merely that you refuse to listen – you are simply not available to take in anything more. You might even prefer to take more on yourself and labour under a great weight of responsibility, to block out the messages of change.

Hexagram 22, *Beauty*

Key Questions

How can you make the essence visible to others?
What do you choose to communicate?

Oracle

'Beauty. Creating success.
Small yield from having a direction to go.'

This is about natural beauty, like the beauty of a plant, whose form is the perfect, simple expression of its nature. It's also about the way people create images to communicate something of a person's or thing's inner nature.

This becomes a fruitful way to engage with the world when you have a purpose in mind – like someone who becomes a suitor for the sake of his bride, or a figure of authority for the sake of those she teaches. This is an image created for the sake of communication and relationship, as a first step towards a chosen destination.

Yet it only bears a 'small yield' because it is only a first, small step. Becoming something for someone is not sufficient to bring about significant results on its own – it's not the same as wholehearted conviction, or ultimate fulfilment. No created image could ever express a whole person.

So this is not a time to concentrate on results: it's a time for imaginative, lively exploration of beautiful ways the essence could flower and be seen.

Image

'Below the mountain is fire: Beauty.
A noble one brings light to the many standards, but does not venture to pass judgement.'

Perhaps the firelight is flickering over the rock face, creating shifting patterns of light and dark. Or perhaps this is the volcanic fire inside a mountain, still dynamically shaping what appears so solid and established from the outside.

The inner light of awareness shines through the outer form, so a noble one sees all the standards, all the ways the world is governed and ordered, from the inside. He understands how things are defined, and how standards arise, and how many forms the inner essence can take. So where could he possibly stand to pass judgement?

Sequence

Beauty follows from Hexagram 21, Biting Through:

'Things cannot carelessly unite and be completed, and so Beauty follows. Beauty means adorning.'

Merely bringing things together is not enough to create true unity; just getting to the truth is not an end in itself. These things will have no real presence in the world – no-one will be able to see or relate to them – until they are fully and carefully expressed.

CHANGING LINES

Line 1 *'Making your feet beautiful.*
Putting away the carriage and going on foot.'

Putting away the carriage means you are not looking for a shortcut and will not force the pace. You don't expect to be whisked away from the dust of the road straight into a ready-made relationship; you're willing to be present on the ground for every step.

You're not laying claim to any special status – and this makes your humility and honest commitment very clear. Naturally, it also means that your progress towards your destination will be slow – but you will have the chance to discover the landscape on the way.

Line 2 *'Making your hair beautiful.'*

You can oil and treat your hair to encourage it to grow and make the most of what you have, but you can't conjure it into instant fullness. You can't act on this situation directly and bring about instant change. This may leave you feeling frustrated and disconnected – but since things can only grow at their own pace, all you can do is to take care of them and wait patiently for the changes to show.

Luxuriant hair is a sign of maturity and vigour. Your hair's growth and health is a true reflection of your inner vitality, so paying attention to it also represents nurturing your own growth into a visibly mature, confident self.

Line 3 *'Beautiful, as if dipped in water.*
Ever-flowing constancy, good fortune.'

Dipping something in water gives it a glossy sheen that brings out the natural brilliance of its colours. Plunging deeply and swiftly into an experience can bring out its beauty and intensity. But for this to mean good fortune, you need to remain true to yourself as well as to the beauty revealed by the water, to retain your personal integrity even in the moment where you are most fully immersed. Don't drown in your imaginings; stay aware of what you're accepting into yourself, and why. You can swim with the river's current without dissolving into it.

Line 4 *'Beautiful like pure white,*
Like a soaring white horse.
Not a robber, but a marital ally.'

A beautiful, dazzling energy makes its entrance, like a suitor coming for his bride with his glossy horses in all their finery. This is a time to express conviction, get started and explore. New possibilities shine brightly; there is the power of a fine horse to lend them momentum as they get underway.

It's hard to see what substance there might be beneath this gleaming white; you might suspect it a fake, come to steal your time and energy. But this is just the nature of the energy at hand: it's for lighting up beginnings, not all the subtler nuances to come. You will not lose anything in the encounter, and there is the potential for great gains – in clarity of intention, in energy, and in expansion through partnership.

Line 5 *'Beauty in a hilltop garden.*
A roll of silk: small, so small.
Shame.
In the end, good fortune.'

The suitor brings a roll of silk as a betrothal gift, but he is embarrassed by how small it is. You seek to make a vital connection, to join with something or someone important to you, but you feel inadequate and ashamed of how little you have to offer. But these things you are concerned about are only superficial, and only temporary. Your authenticity and commitment are far more important.

Line 6 *'White beauty.*
No mistake.'

White beauty is pure and simple with nothing added. Like undyed cloth or a blank canvas, it is ready to take on the colour of the moment. This could be the sign of inner quality and light too modest to draw attention to itself; it could be a self-protective reflex, trying to avoid injury by remaining inconspicuous. But now there is no need for bright dyes or disguises. Even if your experience so far suggests otherwise, you, in your honest presence and commitment, are enough.

Hexagram 23, *Stripping Away*

Key Questions

What has worn out?
Is there a less painful way to let this go?
What is underneath the surface?

Oracle

'Stripping away.
Fruitless to have a direction to go.'

The surfaces are cut and sliced away; the old and unviable is stripped back to expose the living core. This inevitable, natural process often feels like a flaying: the more you have invested of yourself in these old things, the more painful it will be.

It's no good, at such times, to imagine the future and make plans. You need to bring your energy back to the centre and honour the process: this is a time to be transformed, not to act.

Moreover, until the old is so utterly stripped from you that you have *no choice* but to think in new ways, you will only be able to re-create the old patterns.

Image

'Mountain rests on the earth: Stripping Away.
The heights are generous, and there are tranquil homes below.'

The mountain is continually stripped away through erosion, and the valley below it, enriched with fertile soil, becomes a peaceful place for life and growth.

This is a picture of 'stripping away' at its highest potential: as a constant, gradual, natural and painless process. Everything that is built up — power, or achievement, or the edifice of self and identity — must continually erode away. It leaves behind an enriched inner world, and a quiet sense of being at home here.

Sequence

Stripping Away follows from Hexagram 22, Beauty:

'Involved in brightening the appearance; this means success will be truly exhausted, and so Stripping Away follows.'

Creating a true image and expression of the inner essence is good, necessary work. But when that essence has left, expending more energy trying to prop up the old image is futile and exhausting.

Pair

Stripping Away forms a pair with Hexagram 24, Returning:

'Stripping away: rotten. Returning: turnaround.'

Dead wood is pruned back with a sharp knife, and sap returns to the living root for new growth. When the old things end, a new direction opens up and a new cycle begins.

CHANGING LINES

Line 1 *'Stripping away the bed by way of its supports.*
To disregard constancy: pitfall.'

The stable, secure thing you rest on is undermined; its foundations, that supported and validated your inner knowledge, are taken away.

The great danger here is of ignoring that inner knowledge altogether, devaluing it in an anxious search for external confirmation. When external supports are taken away, this is a time to honour your autonomy, your principles, and what you *know*, all the more.

Line 2 *'Stripping away the bed by way of its frame.*
To disregard constancy: pitfall.'

Your resting-place is undermined; the boundaries and differences that give you a distinct, secure adult identity are taken away. This can be profoundly disorientating: there is no reassurance to be had about where you stand, or where you're headed, or whether you're making any progress.

Yet the real danger here lies not just in losing your boundaries, but in disregarding constancy. There is a simpler, deeper, inner way of knowing who and where you are, one that doesn't depend on external reassurances. Now is the time to honour it.

Line 3 *'Stripping away. No mistake.'*

You are connected with an individual, a group or an environment that isn't good for you, and it is not wrong to have this connection stripped away. The situation is simple enough, however complex the emotions around it. Undergoing this 'stripping away' will leave you more centred and less vulnerable.

Line 4 *'Stripping the bed by way of the flesh.*
Pitfall.'

The 'pruning' process goes too far; it cuts away not only support and security, but even living flesh.

This is a danger when you only see the situation in 'positive' terms, always looking for ways to get the best possible outcome. When you place too much emphasis on a narrow definition of 'success', you become blind to the harm you could do.

Line 5 *'String of fish*
Through the favour of the palace people.
Nothing that does not bear fruit.'

There is a gift from the palace people: dried fish, strung together, storing up good fortune. This is a modest gift in itself, not necessarily what you expected or hoped for. But it is a real one, and it promises to be worthwhile.

You can benefit from connections – between people, between past and present, between ideas. With an overview of the situation, you can start to 'string things together' and see a coherent significance in events.

Line 6 *'A ripe fruit uneaten.*
Noble one gets a cart,
Small people strip their huts.'

Here at the end of Stripping Away there is a resource unused and potential untouched. The ripe fruit will naturally, painlessly, 'strip itself away' from the tree; the seeds it contains will germinate and begin new growth, if they find their way to clear ground.

Are you responding like the noble one, or the small people?

A noble one is resourceful and imaginative, and keeps the long-term potential in view. Noble people find the means to move on freely and decisively, away from the destruction of the old, into open fields where that potential can be realized.

Small people are immobile, confined to one place, unable to see future possibilities. They may try to hold on to what was theirs, but their actions are essentially self-destructive, and only hasten the inevitable 'stripping away' of a shelter that was already crumbling.

Hexagram 24, *Returning*

Key Questions

What is just beginning to germinate?
How can you follow your sense of direction more closely?
Where might the path lead now?

Oracle

'Returning, creating success.
Going out, coming in, without anxiety.
Partners come, not a mistake.
Turning around and returning on your path.
The seventh day comes, you return.
Fruitful to have a direction to go.'

Your journey leads you out and home again, through the turning points on your way. Vigour and authenticity return in the still moments of those turning points; life regenerates from the roots, and light returns.

By walking constantly to and from your source, you participate in a two-way flow of creation. You go out and rediscover your own way; you return through an open door to your home and relationships. This is a living motion, like breathing, that revitalizes and restores. Relaxed and spacious, it allows time for the path's natural meanderings, never creating resistance.

Since you are in motion, helpers of all kinds come – travelling companions who walk alongside you for a while. (If someone is meant to be with you, you will never need to leave your path to chase after them.) Just as any road can be travelled in two directions, your path also leads both out and back again, and so – in the fullness of time and following a natural progression – there comes a moment to turn round.

Through all this going and coming and starting afresh, it is good to have an overarching direction and purpose to guide you. The quality of Returning is alive, growing and dynamic – a good time to rediscover your own deepest intent and its harmony with the Dao.

Image

'Thunder dwelling in the centre of the earth: Returning.
The ancient kings closed the borders at winter solstice.

Itinerant merchants did not travel,
The prince did not tour the regions.'

In winter, nothing moves or grows: thunder dwells quietly at the centre of the earth. When spring comes, it will surge up and rouse everything to new life. But at present, it is barely beginning to stir: winter solstice, darkest moment of the year, is when light just begins to return.

The ancient kings cared for their people as the earth covers a dormant seed. They contained people's impulse to rush out and resume business as usual, so that the energy for growth would not be squandered in the depths of winter. This is the turning point on your path, a moment to be still and turn inward to listen for little glimmerings and inklings of awareness, to nurture the seeds of a personal sense of direction.

Sequence

Returning follows from Hexagram 23, Stripping Away:

'Things cannot be completely used up. Stripping Away comes to an end on the outside, and there is turnaround on the inside, and so Returning follows.'

After the last firm line leaves the sixth place of Hexagram 23, it returns in the first place of Hexagram 24, on the inside. Things move in cycles: whenever old growth is stripped away, it is making space for new shoots.

CHANGING LINES

Line 1   *'Not far away, returning - no regrets here.*
               From the source, good fortune.'
This is all part of Returning's journey, and the turnings of the path always bring you back to its source – if you need to change direction, you'll soon be set right. You don't have far to go to return; indeed, you're still on your path, it's just that the path can be travelled both ways.

So there is no need for bitterness or mourning over destinations not reached. Don't let your energy be caught in regrets; allow it to take root again in the field of real possibilities. You don't need to rush into action now and make things happen, but only to turn round and come back to the source.

Line 2   *'Rest and return - good fortune.'*
You don't need to make anything happen now. You can take time to breathe and bring your energy back

to your roots. Nothing will be lost, and you will recover a sense of your own strength and autonomy.

Line 3 *'Repeated returning.*
Danger, no mistake.'

The road home is not a smooth one: there are constant distractions, interruptions and setbacks, so that you never quite gather enough momentum for steady progress. Yet you keep on coming back, covering the same ground and gravitating towards the same place.

The danger here lies less in the travelling to and fro than in the deep-seated anxieties this can awaken. When you see meaning only in the setbacks, overlooking the significance of your constant returning, it's easy to feel discouraged to the point of exhaustion. You can cede so much power to the things that turn you back that you risk losing your own bearings.

Yet the repeated returning is not a mistake: you are returning to your right place, and you may find that with each re-commitment you are gaining in skill and insight.

Line 4 *'Walking in the centre, returning alone.'*

This is a balanced, naturally moderate way of moving, coming from your centre. You wake up to your inner guidance and begin to act accordingly: going at your own pace, in your own direction, heeding your own intuition. This often means moving away from a group towards solitude, following an inner standard, no longer moved by others' influence or expectations.

Line 5 *'Great-hearted return – no regrets.'*

Returning calls for an honest generosity of spirit – for you to be able to relinquish a chosen route while staying loyal to the journey, and to allow all things and people to find their own way.

This is how you change direction without regrets: not wishing yourself elsewhere, but fully inhabiting the present moment – always the only possible turning point. There may be inner and outer resistance to such change, but *precedent is not all-powerful* and patterns can be broken. The living energy at your core is stronger than mere inertia.

Line 6 *'Confused return, pitfall. There is calamity and blunder.*
Using this to mobilize the armies: in the end there is great defeat.
For your state's leader, disaster.
For ten years, incapable of marching out.'

You try to return, but you are lost – your vision distorted by your hungers and fears until you see only a mirage of what you most need to be real. The time for return has gone by; you cannot renew what is past. Maybe this is because of obstinacy and missed opportunities; maybe it is only because the cycle turned.

In any case, it's time now for a completely different path: no amount of energy expended can possibly turn what is past into a prediction of what is to come. If you try to recapture the irretrievable, you will be like the ruler who leads his country into disastrous wars, crippling its powers of regeneration for years to come.

Hexagram 25, *Without Entanglement*

Key Questions

What is real?
What is genuinely your responsibility, and what is not yours at all?

Oracle

'Without entanglement.
Creating success from the source, constancy bears fruit.
One who is not upright commits blunders,
And it is fruitless to have a direction to go.'

To be entangled is to be caught up in futile, groundless things: deluded beliefs, or reckless actions, or a compulsion to rewrite the past or control the future. When you are without entanglement, you recognize what is *not yours*, and you will not take it on. Sometimes other people's problems are not yours to solve; sometimes bad things happen to you and are not your responsibility.

Freedom from entanglement brings extraordinary energy. It liberates the whole creative flow, from source to enduring fruition, natural and spontaneous as a growing plant. This is the creative potential latent in the present moment. To connect with it, you need to be conscious of your place on the earth, and set yourself straight accordingly. Entanglements are groundless; if you realign your course with present reality, you are well grounded. If you don't, you will make bad mistakes.

Now is a good time to re-evaluate your plans, dreams and goals: imagining new places to go is of no use if you can't see where you are — and in any case, even the clearest of plans is not immune to chance.

Image

'Below heaven, thunder moves. All things interact Without Entanglement.
The ancient kings, with abundant growth in accord with the seasons, nourished the ten thousand things.'

Those who are without entanglement are like the natural world: effortlessly in harmony with the quality of the time, connected to the natural movement of heaven with the immediacy of thunder. The ancient kings could nourish the whole world with the abundance of seasonal growth, without ever *making* anything grow.

Sequence

Being Without Entanglement follows from Hexagram 24, Returning:

'Returning, and so truly Without Entanglement.'

If you come back to your own path and calmly follow where it leads, naturally you will be free from entanglement. First you nurture your inner sense of the Way and allow time for this seed to germinate; then you can disentangle from illusion and connect with the underlying truth, and the seed can grow in its season.

Pair

Without Entanglement forms a pair with Hexagram 26, Great Taming:

'Without Entanglement means calamity; Great Taming means the right time.'

Without Entanglement marks a time when bad things can happen through no fault of your own. It is a time to disengage from the misfortune – not yet the right moment to assume ownership of everything in your domain and take action.

CHANGING LINES

Line 1 *'Without entanglement,*
Going on, good fortune.'

When there are obstacles, perhaps when the free flow of communication is blocked, this does not mean it is your job to engage and grapple with the problem. Making progress is not the same thing as clearing blockages – not when you can simply walk past them, disentangled, and move on.

Line 2 *'Not ploughing and reaping, not weeding cleared fields,*
And so then it is fruitful to have a direction to go.'

The endless round of farming chores blurs into a frenzy of work. There would be no use in getting caught up in all that effort without ever clarifying whether it will achieve what you want. After all, you are not your work. So when you stop trying to do everything at once, *then* it will be worthwhile to know your next step – which is as much as you need to know. Then you can go your way both lightly and purposefully, joining with a more potent creative energy.

Line 3 *'The disaster of disentangling.*
Maybe someone tethered a cow –
Travelling people's gain, townspeople's disaster.'

Townspeople identify with their group and want to stay in one place, and also expect what they value to stay where they tether it. But this is an imaginary security. The valuable things of life are like cattle: free-roaming, and quite capable of walking away. Meanwhile, travellers are mobile and flexible; they don't need to own much, and are always on the alert for changes, ready to benefit from the unexpected.

So disentangling brings disaster for the townspeople, while the travellers gain. Which of these are you? And which would you choose to be?

Line 4 *'There can be constancy – no mistake.'*

By disentangling yourself from external influence and the resultant mental clutter, you clear the way for fortitude and independence. You can allow your gifts to flow without interference; you are loyal and persistent. You do not need to be afraid of loss.

Line 5 *'The affliction of disentangling.*
No medicinal herbs, there is rejoicing.'

An anxiety-inducing problem has become a drain on your energy. It's natural to want to sort it out yourself – definitively, and right away. However, for this affliction to be cured, you need first to disentangle from your urge to treat it.

To assume that because there is a problem, it must be your job to intervene, discover and impose a solution, is a very 'entangled' way to be. When you go in search for remedies, you focus on the affliction and prolong the anxiety, instead of simply returning to the native state of health and vigour – which the body already knows, and where this problem does not exist. If you let the natural process follow its course, the problem will resolve itself; there will be rejoicing.

Line 6 *'Without entanglement,*
Acting brings blunders.
No direction bears fruit.'

Being 'without entanglement' has gone too far: someone is going with the flow without thinking and without seeing, failing to commit himself or take charge of developments. He responds to events, drifts with whatever trend is already established, and surrenders his initiative to whatever moves. When he is pulled into action, his cluelessness will be exposed; he is so disengaged that other people's reactions may come as an unpleasant surprise. Intentions make no difference: there is no benefit in planning a route when you don't understand where you are.

Hexagram 26, *Great Taming*

Key Questions

How can you make the most of the potential?
How would it be to master this?

Oracle

'Great taming,
Constancy bears fruit.
Not eating at home, good fortune.
Fruitful to cross the great river.'

The farmer both restrains and controls the energies of nature, and also builds up natural resources and nurtures their growth: he Tames. Great Taming means doing this work with an end in mind – thinking of what can be achieved in future by controlling and accumulating the energies available now. Steady persistence over time, letting each crop complete its growth, will yield good harvests.

This enables you to go beyond your habitual boundaries and nourish yourself on new experience. You can go where more will be asked of you and your gifts will be of greater service; you can sustain values beyond mere survival. The aim is not to achieve perfect control, staying home and accumulating as an end in itself: whatever you accumulate becomes a springboard to new commitments and explorations. Great Taming cultivates the resources for life on a larger scale.

Image

'Heaven dwells in the centre of the mountain: Great Taming.
A noble one uses the many annals of ancient words and past deeds,
And builds up his character.'

Heaven, the creative force, dwells at the centre of what it creates. The present contains the principle and energy that shaped it, and all this is available in the store of memory and written words. A noble one goes into this mountain cave of treasures to read and absorb, cultivating his own quality of character and personal power.

Sequence

Great Taming follows from Hexagram 25, Without Entanglement:

'Being Without Entanglement, hence capable of Taming, and so Great Taming follows.'

To be fully engaged with present opportunity, you must first be fully disentangled from the past. You need to be free from all the things that are not yours to work on before you can make the most of those that are – you disengage in order to re-engage wholeheartedly.

CHANGING LINES

Line 1 *'There is danger.*
Fruitful to stop it.'

Before you can set any intentions or begin a new phase of growth, you must put a stop to whatever is bringing you into danger. If there is a process underway, bring it to a halt. If you are making plans, desist.

By stopping, you give yourself the time to become aware of hidden dangers and interrupt any self-perpetuating patterns. You regain conscious control of your direction. This is a vital preparation for Great Taming – not only because you need to know you are safe before you can concentrate on cultivation, but also because self-mastery is founded on the ability to stop.

Line 2 *'The cart's axle straps come loose.'*

Hidden away under the cart, simple leather straps hold the axles to the body. You might not give these much thought – until they come loose, and the cart falls apart beneath you.

Perhaps ideas and desires have parted company from what is possible. Perhaps your concept of yourself is no longer connected with reality, or inner essence is divorced from its expression. But something essential is broken, and you cannot move on until it is repaired. The drive to make progress may be stronger than ever, but pulling harder when the wheels have come off does not help. Running repairs are not a sensible option, nor is a temporary fix. You will need to stop for a while and have patience.

Yi has nothing to say about whether this is good or bad; it is how it is. Perhaps you could try seeing this enforced halt as an opportunity – to rest and reflect, to choose your direction, and to design a stronger structure, where image, emotion, reality and action are bound together into an integrated, coherent whole.

Line 3 *'A fine horse for pursuit.*
Constancy in hardship bears fruit.
Daily training, chariot driving, protecting.
Fruitful to have a direction to go.'

Before you think about what you are pursuing, you need to concentrate on how you pursue it. The energy and spirit you have for this are of great potential value, like a fine horse. And you cannot have a horse without a duty of care – nor yet a fine, well-trained horse unless you accept the daily work (and discomfort, struggle and sacrifice) of training it. Through constancy, the work becomes the gift.

The horse will follow its instincts and run with the herd. For your power to pursue to become a strength rather than a liability, these impulses must be restrained, boundaries safeguarded and energies redirected – so that *you* control the direction of travel.

Having your chosen direction in mind gives you the motivation to train a fine horse. But what you are really mastering here is freedom of movement, so that it becomes meaningful to choose a direction to go.

Line 4 *'Young bull's hornboard.*
From the source, good fortune.'

You could never overcome a bull in a battle of strength – but you can control it nonetheless, and even turn it into an asset, by using your intelligence, taking the long view, and starting while it's young. By tying a hornboard to a bullock's head, you can keep it from ever learning to use its horns.

Also, tying on a hornboard marks the bullock out as an exceptionally fine creature, worthy to be used in offering – one to be carefully nurtured and protected. To apply restraint in this way to a young, growing thing is a sign of how much you value it.

Line 5 *'Gelded pig's tusks.*
Good fortune.'

A gelded pig will not injure others or damage its own tusks by fighting. It is disarmed, not by removing the tusks, but by removing the impulse to fight. In the same way, you can take the potential for injury out of a situation by removing its emotional charge. What is left is gentler and simpler; it can be modestly practical and still beautiful, and grows into its potential in the course of time.

Line 6 *'Is this heaven's highway?*
Creating success.'

The way is open for heaven's power to travel through the earth. All the energy of Great Taming is released, and the currents of change flow faster, deeper and more powerfully. It's beyond your capacity to understand where this is going, much less control it; all you can know is that it is strong and true and you can have confidence in it. There is no security to be had in trying to stop this; only those who move with it will flourish.

Hexagram 27, *Nourishment*

Key Questions

What would nourish you?
How is your hunger motivating you?
If you accept this as nourishment, who will you become?

Oracle

'Nourishment: constancy brings good fortune.
See the jaws,
Your own quest for something real to fill your mouth.'

Literally, this hexagram is called 'Jaws': it means not only what you eat, but all the processes and structures that sustain nourishment. It includes all forms of nourishment: physical, social, emotional, intellectual, spiritual… all creating and re-creating an individual 'ecosystem' to sustain and shape you.

Constancy brings good fortune: steady, clear persistence in honouring what truly sustains you. Yi calls on you to see the jaws – to become aware. How do you habitually nourish yourself and others? What deep instincts are at work here? What real nourishment are you seeking?

Image

'Below the mountain is thunder: Nourishment.
A noble one reflects on his words in conversation,
And is discriminating about what he eats and drinks.'

The sound of thunder under the mountain echoes and re-echoes, and is slow to fade away. The words you speak are the same: you put them into circulation, and they become part of the constant flow of nourishment among people – the same flow that nourishes you, in the end.

A noble one pays careful attention to both giving and receiving: how he nourishes others, and what he will accept as nourishment from others. You don't have to 'swallow' every opinion you are offered.

Sequence

Nourishment follows from Hexagram 26, Great Taming.

'Things are tamed, and so there can be nurturing, and so Nourishment follows. Nourishment means nurturing.'

Naturally, to nourish people, you need good farmers. The truths you choose to nurture and cultivate in your life become the foundation of your personal ecosystem: they are your basic nourishment, and the energy source for your creative action.

Pair

Nourishment is paired and contrasted with Hexagram 28, Great Exceeding:

*'Nourishment nurtures correctly;
Great Exceeding overbalances.'*

To grow into your whole self, you create a harmonious, balanced cycle of mutual nourishment. Yet this growth will eventually outgrow the framework that sustained it.

CHANGING LINES

Line 1   *'Giving up your own spirit tortoise,
            Gazing at me with jaws hanging down – pitfall.'*
You locate power, meaning and authority outside yourself and gaze at it slack-jawed, expecting someone or something else to provide what you need. You have given up the intrinsic magic of your own nature. What you are depending on is not your true support; it will be stripped away from you.

Line 2   *'Unbalanced nourishment.
            Rejecting the standard, looking to the hilltop for nourishment.
            Setting out to bring order – pitfall.'*
The framework for nourishment is toppling over; the jaws will not meet. Now you seek to reshape the way you receive nourishment, and reject its regular channels and established sources. The 'way things are done', what works day to day, is no longer enough. There's a yearning for something higher, simpler, a more direct connection to the pure source.

In practice, this leaves you between sources of nourishment: rejecting one, and not yet quite reaching

the other. Despite the idealistic impulse of the moment, you need to relinquish any desire to 'fix' things. When your own source of nourishment is out of equilibrium, you're not in any position to set the world to rights.

Line 3 *'Rejecting nourishment – constancy, pitfall.*
For ten years, don't act.
No direction bears fruit.'

This means rejecting nourishment itself – pushing away what you need to live. This could be motivated by a dogmatic adherence to principle; perhaps you're inclined to identify yourself with the principle, as a way to be unique. In any case, this leaves you starving and without resource; it is not ever a good idea, not for any cause.

In fact, it might help to be *without* a cause for a while, and have 'no direction'. If there is no lofty aim in mind, perhaps it might become possible to sense what is needed and what opportunities are open here and now.

Line 4 *'Unbalanced nourishment – good fortune.*
Tiger watches, glares and glares.
Chases and chases his desires.
No mistake.'

When it's time to act on the need for nourishment, you might *need* to be less than perfectly balanced. The tiger succeeds because he is simply a tiger. He sees the world in terms of his appetites, and he pursues them without second thoughts; he is not the model of moderation.

There is nothing wrong with single-mindedly pursuing what you crave. Sometimes you need that intensity, those teeth, to bite through into the essence of things.

Line 5 *'Rejecting the standard,*
Dwelling here with constancy: good fortune.
Cannot cross the great river.'

You reject the established sources and usual channels of nourishment, refuse the way things are always done, aspiring to a richer and broader flow. This is a good time to stay home, not to 'cross rivers' and commit yourself to new adventures. You're not yet capable of sustaining such a commitment – but more than that, there is 'good fortune' from making your home *here*. Perhaps there's nowhere else you need to be?

Line 6 *'Origin of nourishment. Danger, good fortune.*
Fruitful to cross the great river.'

The origin of nourishment – the source it grows from. What you need is right here with you, and responsibility stops here. It's up to you to provide.

There is no safety net to fall back on; you need to be aware of the dangers, and avoid delusions of your own invincibility. But this is also good fortune: because you carry your nourishment with you, you can find your own path again, make new commitments and explore new territory.

Hexagram 28, *Great Exceeding*

Key Questions

What is overloaded?
What have you outgrown?
What must you do?

Oracle

'Great Exceeding, the ridgepole warps.
Fruitful to have a direction to go.
Creating success.'

When you exceed something, you cross over a line and make a transition.

The traditional Chinese house has a structure like an old-fashioned tent: uprights support a horizontal ridgepole, and all the weight of roof and walls is suspended from there. Here, the ridgepole's limits have been exceeded; the supporting framework is no longer adequate to the weight it's asked to bear.

This means stress, and also a greatness of spirit and purpose that goes beyond the scope of the situation. It is fruitful to have a direction to go, to reach out imaginatively and explore. Since things cannot hold up as they are, there *must* be movement.

Image

'The lake submerges the tree: Great Exceeding.
A noble one stands alone without fear,
Withdraws from the time without sadness.'

Water should sustain the tree, but an excess will drown it. Interaction and communication should sustain you, but too much will be overwhelming, drowning the natural growth of your spirit in a flood of demands and expectations. You cannot possibly absorb all these demands and preoccupations into your own identity; you would only lose yourself.

So a noble one is not afraid to stand alone, nor is she depressed at leaving society behind. She is moved by an inner purpose, and not a product of her environment.

Sequence

Great Exceeding follows from Hexagram 27, Nourishment:

'With no nurturance, it is not possible to act, and so Great Exceeding follows.'

Great Exceeding is the opposite experience to Nourishment: imbalance instead of balance, overloading the structure instead of living within it. But to be capable of the dynamic action Great Exceeding requires, you need to be well nourished.

CHANGING LINES

Line 1   *'For the offering mat, use white thatch grass.*
         No mistake.'

Here at the beginning of Great Exceeding, you need to take great care, like someone who cushions their offering with layers of grass. This gentle, generous support is the best way to show your commitment.

     With the roof threatening to fall, you might feel as though you ought to be Doing Something more decisive. Yet in fact, this is the first step: even if the details you attend to are trivial in themselves, what you are caring for is sacred.

Line 2   *'Withered willow sprouts a shoot,*
         Venerable man gets a young wife.
         Nothing that does not bear fruit.'

Willow trees have an irrepressible vitality: the old wood will open to the flow of new sap, and even the withered willow sprouts shoots. And in the same way, even older men can marry and have the chance of new descendants. The framework gains a new lease of life, and nothing fails to bear fruit: even if it seemed exhausted, it can hold space for something new, young and fertile.

Line 3   *'The ridgepole buckles.*
         Pitfall.'

There is too much to bear alone; the ridgepole finds no support, and collapses. Perhaps someone failed to see what support was available; perhaps there was simply none to be found.

Line 4   *'The ridgepole at its peak, good fortune.*
         If there is more, shame.'

The ridgepole high above holds firm; the supporting framework is reinforced; the situation is at its height.

     This means all is well, but also means that the greatest height has already been achieved, and all that is sustainable has already been added. Take care that all you do is supportive, and nothing adds to the burden. If you heedlessly add more stressors, you bring shame down on yourself.

Line 5 *'Withered willow sprouts flowers,*
Venerable woman gets an upright husband.
No blame, no praise.'

The withered willow renews its inner vitality – not with growth, but simply with beauty. The older woman's marriage is the same: she enjoys a real man as husband, even though she's unlikely to bear him children. This is renewal for its own sake; it has nothing to do with future, lasting results.

How to react? Do we enjoy the flowers, or condemn the waste of vital sap? Yi says we can do neither: no blame, no praise. This is beyond the patterns we're familiar with, and cannot be judged.

Line 6 *'Exceeding in wading the river, head underwater.*
Pitfall.
No mistake.'

Going too far as you wade the river, you will be in over your head. You're quite likely to drown.

It's easy to overestimate your ability to handle the unknown, to imagine you can integrate it into your normal life. It can't be done; you can't enter this river without sacrificing at least some part of yourself. Yet even if this is a personal disaster, it is not and cannot be a mistake; it's just how it works when you surrender yourself to the river.

So how far are you prepared to go?

Hexagram 29, *Repeating Chasms*

Key Questions

What are you sure of in your heart when nothing else is sure?
How can you flow on and through the dark?

Oracle

'Repeating chasms.
There is truth and confidence.
Holding your heart fast creates success.
Movement brings honour.'

These are pits, where you fall into the deep, dark waters, flowing on into
the swirling unknowable dark. The chasms repeat: there is no detour that
would take you round them, so you must practise and learn the way of these deep places.

First, there must be truth and confidence: truth to the present moment (because this is simply
how it is) and trust in your inner knowing, so you can be unreservedly present, with an unshakable
grasp on the essential core. In these deep waters, there is nothing solid out there to hold on to –
no external security, no way to orient yourself – and so you hold fast to your heart. This is a way
to create success, staying in communication with creative source even in the chasm.

In movement, you find a different kind of security – one that depends on your heart, courage
and commitment. This is the truest test of your convictions, when you have no way of knowing
where your leaps of faith might land. Sitting in the bottom of the chasm does not bring honour;
action does. Also, it's a way to be sure of yourself as an individual after everything else has fallen
away. You act, and you become skilled in flowing through the steep-sided chasms.

Image

'Waters flow on and reach the end: Repeating Chasms.
A noble one acts with constant character and teaches things by repeating.'

Many small tributaries flow together to create a broad river; many small commitments flow
together to create a powerful character. A noble one understands that just one extraordinary
leap of faith is not enough; by acting consistently, he creates a continuity of principles that people
can depend on when all else is in flux.

Such repetition is a way of conveying a message to others, and sometimes also of convincing and changing yourself as you learn more skilful ways of thinking. This is like the water: it carves out a course and creates its own momentum.

Sequence

Repeating Chasms follow from Hexagram 28, Great Exceeding:

'Things cannot end with excess, and so the Chasm follows. The Chasm means falling.'

In Hexagram 28, the house's ridgepole was buckling; now it has given way. You overburdened, or simply outgrew, the external framework that supported you, and now you are falling.

Pair

Repeating Chasms are paired and contrasted with Hexagram 30, Clarity:

'Clarity is above, the chasm is below.'

These are natural opposites: above and below, fire and water, light and dark, waking and dreaming. Yet together, they create a single landscape. Chinese tradition says that after its journey across the sky, the sun is bathed in the river at the foot of the Leaning Mulberry tree: the sun itself needs to 'repeat the chasm'.

CHANGING LINES

Line 1 *'Repeated chasms.*
Entering into the pit within the chasm – pitfall.'
You need to go *through* chasms, not further down into them. You cannot solve the chasm, or know it, or get the measure of it: you can only get sucked further and further down, into the pit within the chasm.
　　Maybe you've been this way before? It takes you ever further from your centre; you get more and more lost. It won't be at all easy to find your way out again. Now would be a good time to stop digging.

Line 2 *'The chasm has sheer sides. Seek small gains.'*
Down at the bottom of the pit, you aspire to be out in the open where you belong, relating freely and

naturally with others. However, the chasm has sheer sides; you can't escape it in a single bound. So don't try to leap to the perfect conclusion or design the whole picture at once. To travel towards that free and open space, seek only the small gains that are available to you here and now. Travel inward first, and trust your intuition from moment to moment to show the next, small step.

Line 3 *'Coming to chasm on chasm. Sheer sides also a resting place.*
Entering into the pit within the chasm – do not act.'

Down and down you go, and into the depths…

Sometimes it seems as though if you just push a little further in, you'll reach a simple solution. This is a delusion. You're in a deep hole, and there is nothing useful you can do about it now. Put your spade down; take the opportunity to rest. Knowing the limits of what you can do can be a rest in itself.

Line 4 *'A cup of wine, a pair of dishes, using earthenware.*
Let in with ropes from the window. In the end, no mistake.'

Imagine someone isolated in a prison pit, with just a small opening to the world above, and help lowered through the opening. With a link to the world above the pit, there's no longer any need to dig further down.

This is a very simple picture: there's an opening, and a connection, and there is help. It's not much – you may wish it could be more, or faster – but there's really no call for a more elaborate offering. Simplicity and discretion help to ensure the connection can be made smoothly, where grand gestures might alert the guards and trigger a defensive reaction.

Line 5 *'The chasm does not overflow,*
Here it already finds its level – no mistake.'

It's in the nature of water to find its level and become still. It doesn't insist on climbing up out of pools and flowing onward for the sake of 'making progress'.

Offerings to the earth are poured into pits. There comes a moment when your offering has been received and accepted, and then you don't need to pour in any more.

This line speaks of the wisdom of enough. This doesn't mean there is no further to go (there almost always is, after all); it only means that you needn't feel impelled to push things forward by giving more and more. Progress will happen of itself, in due course; for now you can pause, contemplate the possibilities, and allow things to be complete as they are. This is not a mistake: there is nothing you have to do and nowhere else you have to be just now.

Line 6 *'Bound with good rope and cords.*
Shut away in a thorn thicket.
For three years, gains nothing. Pitfall.'

At first, you are bound into relationship, with its ties and limits. The water in the chasm will stay within its limits; this is how it can flow through. But when limits are not observed or bonds not honoured, you are shut away from the flow altogether. Then you are utterly trapped: your confinement will last for the set time, and there is nothing constructive to be done.

Hexagram 30, *Clarity*

Key Questions

What do you see?
What does it mean?
How can you nourish and sustain a high level of awareness?

Oracle

'Clarity. Constancy bears fruit.
Creating success.
Raising female cattle is good fortune.'

The ancient Chinese character for Clarity shows a flying bird, and a net to capture it. Birds are messengers; this one represents flashes of insight, the way things can light up and shine out clearly. We weave a net of concepts to grasp the message and hold its meaning in awareness. This is not passive seeing, but a meeting of outer and inner light.

Seeing the truth and holding to it with constancy bears fruit. Then the moment of insight can become lasting awareness, so that we enter into creative communication with the signs and messages around us, and truly see other people.

Just as a bright light needs fuel, such a level of attention and understanding demands a great deal of energy. Female cattle represent the reserves of strength that sustain awareness, along with a quiet willingness for that strength to be used and guided. They would be the support of an old farming culture, providing both food and power so that the people could develop a higher culture and a better understanding of their world.

So take care of your cattle, and build up your reserves. As well as paying attention to what you see, nurture your capacity to see; cultivate the part of you that shelters and nourishes new insight.

Image

'Doubled light gives rise to Clarity.
Great People with continuous light illuminate the four regions.'

The trigram for fire and light is doubled in this hexagram, both inside and outside. So this is not just a flash of light that vanishes into the gloom, but continuous illumination. The inner awareness

of great people shines out, spreading understanding further and further into the world – perhaps not because of how brightly it burns, but because it is an unbroken stream of light.

Sequence

Clarity follows from Hexagram 29, Repeating Chasms:

'Falling naturally has occasion to hold together, and so Clarity follows.
Clarity means holding together.'

In the chasms, you find nothing solid to catch hold of in the outside world; you're falling, and you must 'hold fast your heart'. When there is nothing else, what you hold on to will be the truth. Light is renewed by the experience of darkness, and clarity arises from emotional depths.

CHANGING LINES

Line 1 *'Treading in confusion.*
Honour it - not a mistake.'

The beginnings of clarity are like waking up. All the options, messages, emotions and responsibilities of the situation flood in on you like an intense light. Life was much less disorientating when you were asleep.

Perhaps you go out in the morning light to see whether spirits in animal form have left traces in the smoothed earth. Even if their tracks are confused and indecipherable, you can see that they visited. You can perceive that there *is* a message here for you, and respect it even though you cannot read it.

In the same way, you can honour the fact that you are in motion yourself, even though the right way to go is not clear and you can only make provisional plans. You don't yet have a context to contain and interpret the messages, and it can be very disconcerting to move before you can see the whole picture. Nonetheless, it is not a mistake to be underway.

Line 2 *'Clear golden light.*
From the source, good fortune.'

The bright radiance of full sunlight is the life-sustaining energy that everything is made of. You know it as an inner light that burns clearly and steadily: it does not blaze up to extremes; it is not showy or dazzling, it simply radiates out evenly into the world.

This is the energy that illuminates your understanding as it circulates endlessly behind and through your emotions – celebration or mourning, attachment and moving on. It exists in motion and is not dependent on a single source, and so it is not extinguished.

Line 3 *'In the clear light of the setting sun,*
If not beating a pot and singing,
Then you will be making the lament of great old age.
Pitfall.'

The sun sets; the world turns; a day comes to its close. This is the end of one phase of your life, and the light of endings colours all you see. It is time to take in what has happened, and move into the present moment. You need to sing your own song, beat your drum and celebrate the achievements of the day. You cannot keep the sun from setting, but this is no reason to feel ineffectual or helpless.

Unless you celebrate deliberately and loudly, you will sink into melancholy, futilely resisting the passing of time, dwelling on what is lost to you as you watch the light and colour fade from your visions.

Line 4 *'Sudden, it comes,*
Burns,
Dies,
Thrown out.'

A tremendously bright light flares up, shines out – maybe beautifully, maybe painfully – and demands attention. And then it dies away and is discarded. This is not good or bad, it's just the nature of a flame that does not have enough fuel to sustain itself for long.

Don't be misled by its brilliance, or set too much store by what you imagine you have seen: it is not as significant as it appears. The glow of images and roles lives just as long as they do, then dies away, and what you see in that brief burst of light is not the complete picture.

Line 5 *'Weeping tears like flowing streams,*
Sad as if in mourning.
Good fortune.'

It is good to see what you have lost, and to mourn it – to let grief flow, like time. And it is good to recognize one another with compassion, and see how transience and loss unite us. Tears cleanse the eyes.

Line 6 *'The king uses this to march out,*
There are honours.
He executes the chief – the captives are not so ugly.
Not a mistake.'

You are learning to see what must be done, and have the motivation and energy to undertake it. Like the king, ready to lead out his army, you have the initiative. You might not want it; it might be easier to have less power and less exposure to the risk of failure. Yet though there seem to be countless problems to deal with, there is only one – a single root cause of the trouble – and all the rest follows.

Rather than misplacing your aggression and wasting your energy in misdirected attacks around the periphery, you need to focus all your powers on seeking out that central cause. You need not worry about leaving other problems unaddressed; they will be disarmed when you succeed at the centre.

Hexagram 31, *Influence*

Key Questions

What influence is active – and what does it draw you towards?
What is its place in your life?

Oracle

'Influence, creating success.
Constancy bears fruit.
Taking a woman, good fortune.'

Influence is what moves people, and how people are open and available
to be moved – by emotion or inspiration, physical responses or visiting spirits. All these things
touch, stir and attract us, drawing us into relationship. The Chinese character for 'influence'
shows a mouth and a weapon: the influence goes deep, and makes us vulnerable.

It is good to respond to the power of influence with constancy, steadying the motion it
inspires and creating a place in your life to contain it. The man who 'takes a woman' in marriage
brings her into his home and makes room for her there. Good fortune comes from this more
feminine way of relating: being open and allowing space for new influences.

Image

'Above the mountain is a lake: Influence.
A noble one accepts people with emptiness.'

The lake can form because the mountain makes space for it, yet still remains inwardly solid. With
solid rock on the inside, there can be clear water above; without it, there would only be mud
throughout.

In the same way, the noble one accepts people into an empty space. He ensures that he can
hear and receive others without confusing his self with theirs.

Sequence

The Yijing is divided into two canons: the Upper Canon ends with Hexagram 30, Clarity, and the

Lower Canon begins here. Influence follows from all the hexagrams that precede it:

'There is heaven and earth, and so there are the ten thousand things.
There are the ten thousand things, and so there is man and woman.
There is man and woman, and so there is husband and wife.
There is husband and wife, and so there is father and son.
There is father and son, and so there is ruler and minister.
There is ruler and minister, and so there is higher and lower.
There is higher and lower, and so there is a place for rites and justice to operate.'

This is a creation story for the human world: how it arises from relationships, beginning with the first two hexagrams and culminating in harmonious ways to relate to people and to the spirits. It sets attraction and influence in context, showing how people belong together and complement one another.

Pair

Influence forms a pair with Hexagram 32, Lasting:

'Influence calls, Lasting endures.'

Influence is a time to be called and moved; it is always an encounter with something new.

CHANGING LINES

Line 1 *'Influence in your big toes.'*
Influence first enters your awareness as a stirring realization that you could be somewhere else. Something is pulling you – and with no clear ideas yet of what it might be, you only know that you have itchy feet.

　　This is not yet good or bad: nothing has happened yet; you are still standing where you were before. But everything *could* happen. Those small toes can set the whole body in motion; even the very beginnings of influence open up the structure of your commitments and relationships for far-reaching transformation.

Line 2 *'Influence in your calves, pitfall.*
　　　　Staying in place, good fortune.'
This is a mindless, muscular energy, ready to bounce into action and start afresh, that may pull you off-balance. Its momentum quickly 'walks' you into bad places you can't so easily escape, wasting your energy

and the situation's positive potential. But if you settle down and put yourself on a more stable footing, any action you take later – after reflection, and from a state of equilibrium – will be stronger. You don't have to use your energy now; being able to move doesn't make it the right time to act. Sometimes *not* acting when the impulse takes you is a powerful way to establish your independence from old patterns.

Line 3 *'Influence in your thighs,*
Holding on to your following
Going on, shame.'

You're moved to run, swiftly and strongly, after your object of desire. You fixate on it and pursue it reflexively, one step following the next faster than thought. Wholly invested in the pursuit, you fail to see the better possibilities around you. Your desire distracts you from what you truly want.

   An essential first step is to get a grip on this 'following': to recognize that this pattern is not good for you, and you need to bring it under control. However, recognition alone is not enough: going on in the same direction, just in a more conscious and 'controlled' way, is shameful. You need a new destination.

Line 4 *'Constancy brings good fortune, regrets vanish.*
Wavering, wavering, going and coming,
Friends follow your thoughts.'

It's time to move on with steadiness of purpose, leaving behind what did or did not happen in the past. This is not an easy step to take, so you find yourself unsettled and indecisive, wavering between options: do you follow precedent, or can you change course?

   Even if it looks like mere vacillation, this to-and-fro motion can actually be the sign of an intuitive process at work, learning the paths between what you're leaving behind and what is to come, and finding a way round obstacles. If you have an overarching purpose and clear direction, you will be supported; otherwise, 'wavering' can become a paralysis of indecision. Helpers of all kinds are ready to go along with your thoughts – which makes it very important to choose where your thoughts are going.

Line 5 *'Influence in the neck and shoulders. No regrets.'*

Your neck and shoulders are both strong and flexible; they control your stance and how you look out on the world. When influence reaches this point, you respond with alert attention to your environment – this imperfect, real world your inspirations must connect with. And when you heed the influence and choose to change direction, you move your neck and shoulders first.

   This influence affects your attitude, but cannot 'run away with you': it forms a strong partnership with your will and purpose. With choices and connections consciously made, there is no call for regrets.

Line 6 *'Influence in your jaws, cheeks and tongue.'*

Words are a way to express an influence while keeping at a safe distance from real action. They are not good or bad; they are simply a way for ideas and feelings to find an outlet with no direct consequences.

   But eloquent words carry emotional power, and have indirect consequences: they magnify and spread the influence that inspired them. Yet they should still not be mistaken for anything more than words.

Hexagram 32, *Lasting*

Key Questions

What inspiration are you making real in your daily life?
How can you continue on the same path, even as you adapt?
Who will you become by persevering in this?

Oracle

'Lasting, creating success.
Not a mistake.
Constancy bears fruit,
Fruitful to have a direction to go.'

Whatever becomes part of the heart's circling journey will last. We bind things – influences, ideas, people – into the fabric of our lives by integrating them into the daily round of our way of living, so that they are carried with us through change.

This is an active creative process, keeping the channels always open for exchange between inspiration and reality. Lasting tirelessly on your own path, whatever landscapes it travels through, is not a mistake.

What lasts bears fruit, not because you 'arrive' at some final destination, but because through all the changes you persevere in your intent and inspiration, and you are always finding ways to make it real.

Image

'Thunder and wind: Lasting.
A noble one stands firm and does not change
his bearings.'

Thunder and wind are endlessly changeable, but they are part of a larger, lasting cycle. The noble one's inner nature, subtle as the wind, translates into action as decisive as thunder. So however the environment changes, everything he does will always travel in the same direction.

Sequence

Lasting follows from Hexagram 31, Influence:

'The way of husband and wife cannot fail to endure, and so Lasting follows. Lasting means enduring.'

Influence is a traditional hexagram for betrothal, and Hexagram 32 for marriage. You are attracted towards something enduring, so influence can be fixed into life like dye into a cloth. Then the lasting patterns of life are infused with vitality.

CHANGING LINES

Line 1 *'Deep into lasting.*
          Constancy, pitfall.
          No direction bears fruit.'

If you plunge deeply and precipitately into something that lasts, it will not be so easy to get out.

At this stage, you have plenty of vigorous energy ready to create a strong, lasting pattern. Yet much as you might like to have things settled, and however persuasive the solution may sound, this is not the moment to commit yourself. If you press on without reflection, you'll be in trouble: diving headlong into a deep hole, unable to plan your way out of it, and facing a real struggle to escape or to make any progress.

Line 2 *'Regrets vanish.'*

Those regrets were for paths not taken, and most especially for ideals left behind. They're part of the journey, and they vanish because you move on: now, instead of dwelling in nostalgic comparisons, you are engrossed in immediate, practical details. Your purpose suffuses daily life; it's no longer experienced as a pure ideal, shining on the horizon of some grand vista, but in the next small step on the road.

Line 3 *'Not lasting in your character,*
          Maybe accepting a shameful gift.
          Constancy: shame.'

Unsure about binding yourself to a personal commitment, with no firm promise to guide your steps, you follow whatever path looks most promising, and doubt and second-guess your decisions as circumstances change.

Whatever rewards you gain this way will feel shameful, because they are not given to your true self – how could they be, when your true self was never completely present? If you don't fully realize the gift of your own self, anything else you receive is tainted by that failure, and cannot be integrated into your path. Carrying on in this way brings humiliation.

Line 4 *'In the field, no game.'*

You're hunting – and what you are hunting for *is not here*. You are in the wrong place; staying here longer won't change that.

You may have a great deal invested in this field, having spent a lot of energy in mapping out a context that *should*, in principle, yield those much-desired results. Nonetheless, there aren't any. This does not mean there is no game anywhere in the world, or that this field is empty of other possibilities – only that if you want to succeed in your search, you will have to move on into a wider landscape beyond it.

Line 5 *'Lasting in your character with constancy.*
For the mature woman, good fortune.
For the young man, pitfall.'

To 'last in your character' is to be consistent, follow through on your commitments and keep your promises. Whether or not this is a good idea depends on what kind of character is involved.

The mature woman knows herself, and works to bring ideas to fruition in lasting results that will be a true image of her nature. This is how she establishes herself in the world.

The young man is still inventing and discovering his character; his nature is still in flux and cannot be circumscribed within relationships and commitments. He may not know where his commitments will lead; he may not even stay the same person he was when he made them. He needs above all to allow space for his character to change, so he isn't forever defined by impulsive, youthful decisions.

Which of these characters might you be, in relation to your question? Or, if you find that you contain aspects of mature woman and young man together, how might they co-exist in better balance?

Line 6 *'Shaking up lasting, pitfall.'*

You're restless; the routine is chafing; you want to be somewhere else and begin a completely new life. But what comes next for you must necessarily evolve from those patterns you're already living: you can only start from here. If you constantly 'start over', always envisioning a new life, never working on the life you have, you will never achieve anything real.

Hexagram 33, *Retreat*

Key Questions

What must you do to stay safe and whole?
How can you change your relationships so they
support your integrity?

Oracle

 *'Retreat, creating success.
Constancy yields a small harvest.'*

The old Chinese character for 'retreat' shows a pig and footsteps on the road; perhaps this pig is
running away so as not to be eaten.

Retreat means withdrawing from what can harm you, or what might swallow you up: it is a
way to keep yourself whole. So retreating creates success: it is not defeat, but the way to avoid
defeat, like an army that falls back and stays intact. When you retreat, you hide yourself away –
you might disappear into the landscape altogether – so that you will not lose yourself.

Retreat moves away from threats, and towards wholeness and integrity. It is a way to be
constant to principle, and to yourself, by paying less attention to immediate results. The army
that is loyal to a longer-term objective will retreat in good order rather than linger to gather
spoils. The hermit, constant to the truth he perceives, withdraws from society into an inner
space; he is not interested in claiming tangible rewards. Such constancy, offering no resistance
and creating no friction, bears fruit in small, inconspicuous ways.

Image

*'Below heaven is the mountain: Retreat.
A noble one keeps small people at a distance,
Not with hatred, but through respect.'*

The mountain stands firm and still, and seems to be joined more with heaven than with earth.
The noble one who retreats up the mountain shares this character – staying close to what
inspires, he is naturally distanced from what would diminish him. This happens through respect

and without hostility, because to hate something is to take the ugliness you perceive into your heart.

Sequence

Retreat follows from Hexagram 32, Lasting:

'They cannot last long in the place where they settle, and so retreat follows. Retreat means withdrawing.'

Perhaps you must retreat from your settled place before you are overrun. Perhaps there comes a time when pattern and routine begin to absorb you completely, so you withdraw before your individuality is subsumed.

Pair

Retreat forms a pair with Hexagram 34, Great Vigour:

'Great Vigour means stopping, Retreat means withdrawing.'

Sometimes you can take a stand and hold your position; sometimes you need to move away.

CHANGING LINES

Line 1 *'Retreating tail, danger.*
Do not use this to have a direction to go.'
As you retreat, your tail is the part of you closest to the threat. There's a danger that you could be caught by the tail and pulled back into trouble – into a situation where you can be harmed, and old patterns and roles can swallow you up altogether. You need to get completely clear of these influences and leave them far behind before you can safely make plans for the future; at present, trying to envisage the new makes you vulnerable to being drawn back into old dangers.

Line 2 *'Using yellow rawhide to bind it,*
It will never be capable of getting loose.'
You retreat because you do not want to lose yourself; you are trying to get to a safe distance from anything

that could harm you. And yet there are some possibilities you value and do not want to leave behind.

So how can you find a balance – retreat safely, and yet not lose that creative potential? You can hold on to it strongly as you retreat, with rawhide that contracts as it dries and tightens the bonds. It will not be lost to you, but neither can it take control and endanger your retreat.

Line 3 *'Tied retreat. There is affliction, danger.*
Nurturing servants and handmaidens, good fortune.'

Ties make it hard to retreat; they stress and weaken you with fears of being trapped. You are in danger of being pulled back and eaten up. So it is time to build up a reserve of your own, which will serve and support you in retreating. (Maybe you could even transform the nature of the ties themselves.)

This is not a way to accomplish anything grand: communication is not flowing freely enough to allow that. It is simply a way to be more resourceful, so that your retreat is well provided-for and consequently what ties you and pulls you back no longer exerts the same power. This can make your retreat easier, and even enjoyable.

Line 4 *'Loving retreat.*
Noble one, good fortune.
Small people, blocked.'

You retreat out of love and respect, to allow space and freedom for yourself and all involved. You avoid pointless confrontation, and – again out of love and respect for the integrity of all involved – you will no longer try to force things to work. It is a sign of strength, and of a higher, more imaginative kind of commitment, to withdraw and seek something more natural and fitting.

Small people cannot see this longer view, though, and so they only experience the retreat in terms of what is taken from them or denied them. However, they lack influence here, and cannot prevent the retreat.

Line 5 *'Praiseworthy retreat.*
Constancy, good fortune.'

You are right to retreat. There is nothing you truly need from the position you're in; by retreating you recapture your independent identity and stay loyal to your own path. You are not merely retreating from a threat, but *towards* your own purpose, and so you are moving onto firmer ground.

In leaving you are being true to yourself; however, this does not make it comfortable or easy. You will need to be steady and persistent, and keep your reasons in mind.

Line 6 *'Rich retreat.*
Nothing that does not bear fruit.'

In the end, retreating enriches you – with confidence, with future promise, and above all with a sense of your own independence. Because you know you are self-sufficient, you are less vulnerable, and not easily influenced, and your communication becomes calmer and more self-possessed. It is safe for you to be open and enriched by the world.

Hexagram 34, *Great Vigour*

Key Questions

How will you use your power?
Where do you stand?

Oracle

 'Great Vigour,
Constancy bears fruit.'

With Great Vigour, you stand upright and robust, full of resilient energy. You are inspired and animated by strong purpose, and ready to wield your strength like a hero.

For this to yield results, you will need to act with steadiness and consistency – standing in your strength, but without mistaking it for omnipotence.

Image

'Thunder dwells above heaven: Great Vigour.
A noble one treads no path that is without ritual.'

The action of thunder rests on the underlying principles of heaven. The noble one, acting with Great Vigour, will not be improvising and adapting as he goes along: such great energy needs better guidance if it is to avoid injury. He follows ritual – that is, he acts in ways that observe the principles of creation, and follows their patterns. It is not so much a matter of 'respecting the rules' for their own sake, as of respecting what is known to work, because it is in harmony with the nature of things.

Sequence

Great Vigour follows from Hexagram 33, Retreat:

'Things cannot end with retreat, and so Great Vigour follows.'

In Retreat, you withdraw to preserve your integrity and strength. But when you are strong, you cannot stay invisible forever. Instead of withdrawing, you stand firm.

CHANGING LINES

Line 1   *'Vigour in the toes.*
Setting out to bring order: pitfall.
There is truth and confidence.'

It's as if you were bouncing on the balls of your feet, full of nervous energy, eager to get underway and start making things happen.

The problem is that vigour in your toes is not at all the same thing as clarity in your vision. You know, absolutely, the intensity of your own feeling; you do not have the same understanding of your changing environment.

If you forge ahead regardless, it will all come to grief; acting merely because you *can* act is not a good guiding principle. It is enough to be aware, sure and true here and now, without trying to bring your world into order.

Line 2   *'Constancy, good fortune.'*

The demands and opportunities of the moment can be overwhelming. Steady yourself; remember your purpose – it is stronger than the circumstances, and so are you.

Put your principles into practice, all the time, all your life.

Line 3   *'Small people use vigour,*
Noble one uses a net.
Constancy: danger.
The ram butts a hedge,
Entangles his horns.'

Here are two ways you could engage with an awkward situation.

There is the noble one's way, using a net. He senses the currents of the situation, allows what he does not want to pass him by without resistance, and waits patiently. He can see that the most direct approach is not necessarily the easiest.

And there is the way of the small person, who lacks in imagination and applies all the power he has, just because he can. This is not a safe option in the long run: forging ahead by main strength alone, determined and blind to circumstances, sooner or later he will encounter an immovable limit. The ram only discovers these by challenging the hedge and exhausting his power.

Line 4 *'Constancy, good fortune.*
Regrets vanish.
The hedge is broken through, no entanglement.
Vigour in the axle straps of a great cart.'

Persistence pays off. The barriers that trapped you are overcome; the past and all its patterns are left behind. You break through with no loss of momentum and are not weakened.

How does this become possible? Not through the power of the horses or the weight of the cart, but through the flexible, supple strength hidden away in the axle straps. These are the connections that hold everything together – like for example the connection between what you know and what you do – and allow the strength you exert to translate into continuous forward movement. Invigorate connections, and you can break free.

Line 5 *'Losing sheep at Yi.*
No regrets.'

There are some things you cannot hold on to; they are not permanently, securely yours. Change happens ('Yi' means 'change'), they are lost to you, and you move on – and by moving on, you keep yourself in one piece.

What you once valued disappears from your life, and yet you find you are still yourself, essentially undiminished by the loss; through such change, you determine who you are. In the end, you may even find that your strength is greater than before.

Line 6 *'The ram butts the hedge.*
Cannot pull back, cannot follow through,
No direction bears fruit.
Hardship, and hence good fortune.'

The ram has confused reaching his goal with forcing his way through the hedge. He never imagined that there might be another way round, and has reduced the whole situation to the question of how much power he has. He is strong, overconfident, and in a hurry. Unfortunately, when he charges headlong into a battle of strength with the hedge, he loses.

The hedge is made of a thorny tangle of circumstances, and inflexible thinking will keep you stuck there. The more strongly you charge in, the more stuck you get; getting out will be much harder than getting in. Neither forcing your way forward nor wrenching back will help, but if you do not choose a direction at all, and instead feel your way round each tangle in turn, you will eventually work your way free.

This hard experience brings good fortune – not only freedom, but also a new clarity of insight.

Hexagram 35, *Advancing*

Key Questions

What gifts and opportunities have you been given?
How can you make the most of them?

Oracle

'Advancing, Prince Kang used a gift of horses to breed a multitude. In the course of a day, he mated them three times.'

Prince Kang was the brother of Wu, the Martial King who became first ruler of the Zhou dynasty. He supported him faithfully, and Wu rewarded him with a gift of horses.

So when you are like Kang, you have remarkable gifts of strength and inspiration: gifts as beautiful as horses, that enable you to travel further and faster. You are popular; you are blessed.

Kang did not just sit back and admire his horses; he worked intensively to multiply them and magnify the gift. To be truly blessed, you need to act accordingly; to advance and prosper, you need to seize all you are given as an opportunity.

Image

'Light comes forth over the earth: Advancing.
A noble one's own light shines in her character.'

The light emerging over the earth is like sunrise. Just as the sun appears to be daily renewed and sustained by the earth, so the noble one's light emerges from her character, which is the 'earth' she's made of. Her inner quality, her willingness to give and receive, sustains the shining light in everything she does.

Sequence

Advancing follows from Hexagram 34, Great Vigour:

'Things cannot be completed with vigour, and so Advancing follows. Advancing means making progress.'

It is not enough just to be strong and stand firm. You will want to make the most of the strength you have, and make it mean something by putting it to use.

Pair

Advancing forms a pair with Hexagram 36, Brightness Hidden:

'Advancing means daylight, Brightness Hidden means castigation.'

Now, you are the one who is popular, blessed and bathed in sunlight; sometimes, you are the one who is punished, pursued and cast out into the dark.

CHANGING LINES

Line 1   *'Now advancing, now stopped.*
          Constancy, good fortune.
          A net for truth and confidence,
          Abundant, no mistake.'

You start out full of energy, ready and willing to make progress – and you are abruptly brought to a standstill. It's hard not to react to such frustration by either fighting or fleeing, but if instead you engage with the obstacle with steady determination, you can get past it.

   Meeting resistance in this way gives you pause; it creates space where you can apprehend the true opportunity and gift in the situation – like a net that, without moving, catches fish while the water flows on through. You may have been stopped, but you are still rich.

Line 2   *'Now advancing, now apprehensive.*
          Constancy, good fortune.
          Accepting fine armour,
          Blessing from your ancestral mother.'

As you make progress, you face a transition, and feel anxious and uncertain about what comes next. Going on steadily will bring good fortune: you receive a gift of protection and security that sets limits to your anxiety and becomes a mantle of confidence.

   The gift comes as a blessing from an ancestor, a grandmother, perhaps a queen; whether or not you meet her, you know someone is watching over your well-being.

Line 3 *'All have confidence. Regrets vanish.'*

To experience a consensus in your support – a wholehearted affirmation of what you understand and aspire to – is a powerful gift. As you gather confidence, from both outer and inner sources, you build the capacity to move on with your journey, letting regrets fade away behind you.

Line 4 *'Advancing like a long-tailed rodent,*
　　　Constancy: danger.'

This rodent advances in an opportunistic way by taking what it needs and hiding it away in its own little pile, scurrying from one grain to the next. Although it constantly scuttles around the perimeter of the huge grain store, it is too small to see anything so large. It represents a myopic mentality, without greater purpose, always feeling threatened and exposed, and motivated primarily by the fear of loss.

In its own way, the rodent advances and prospers. There might be times when it is better to advance like a rodent, on a small, manageable scale, than not to advance at all. There must be an end to this, though: to persist in such small-scale thinking is dangerous. Fearful motivation and limited perspective will undermine you and warp your tactics; the smaller you act, the smaller you become.

Line 5 *'Regrets vanish.*
　　　Letting go, gaining, do not worry.
　　　Going on is good fortune,
　　　Nothing that does not bear fruit.'

Not everything is going to work out. Not all people are always honourable, kind and positive. Consequently, your best efforts will not always be justly rewarded with success – and this is not a sign that the world is broken and you must mend it.

Let your regrets go, for everything lost and every apparent opportunity that wasn't quite realized. Find an overview that puts gain and loss into perspective, and do not use them as a personal scorecard: you have better measures of your true progress. You do what you can, let it be, and move on – and you are that much richer and more alive because you're in motion.

Line 6 *'Advancing with your horns.*
　　　Holding fast, use this to subjugate the city.
　　　Danger, good fortune, not a mistake.
　　　Constancy: shame.'

You tap into your strongest motivation, throw your whole self into the effort and charge headlong for your goal. You may not have any very clear idea of how to direct your energy, but you hold fast to your objective and refuse to let it go. At least you will not miss any opportunity for lack of trying.

This kind of approach can be used to attain a single, central, personal goal: something specific that is within your own realm. It's dangerous, but you use that to spur yourself into determined action and break through fear or self-doubt. However, this is only a short-term tactic; to adopt the horns-first approach in the long term would be shameful.

Hexagram 36, *Brightness Hidden*

Key Questions

When no one is looking, who are you?
How do you safeguard that light?

Oracle

'Brightness hidden.
Constancy in hardship bears fruit.'

In the last days of the Shang dynasty as it fell into corruption, Prince Ji was one of the very few virtuous men remaining at court. Remonstrating with the ruler would invite brutal retributions; to flee would be a shameful desertion.

The story goes that once, the king and his entourage were so drunk they literally didn't know what day it was. Messengers were sent to ask Ji. Rather than reveal himself as the only one who knew, he feigned drunkenness and madness. In this way he was able to survive through the last days of Shang without compromising his principles by cooperating with the regime.

'Brightness Hidden' also means 'Brightness Wounded'. Since others do not share your standards or insight, it would be dangerous to let the light of your character shine out freely. Perhaps you have been injured; perhaps you fear injury. Yet you cannot, or will not, leave the situation in search of a stronger position. Instead, you stay true to the light and keep it burning in these hard times by hiding it away.

Image

'Brightness enters the earth's centre: Brightness Hidden.
A noble one, overseeing the crowds, uses darkness and light.'

Light enters the earth's centre at night. The sun will rise again in the morning; the darkness is simply part of a natural cycle. The noble one understands and uses it as such, in balance with light. There is no need to let the full glare of your insight shine forth all the time, or to force your understanding on those who might not want it.

Sequence

Brightness Hidden follows from Hexagram 35, Advancing.

'Advancing necessarily has occasion for injury, and so Brightness Hidden follows;
Brightness Hidden means injury.'

As you progress faster, shine more brightly and expect more from yourself and from life, you naturally become more vulnerable.

CHANGING LINES

Line 1   *'Brightness hidden, flying away,*
His wings hanging down.
The noble one is on the move,
For three days, eats nothing,
Has a direction to go.
Those in authority have something to say.'

You are in flight like a tired, wounded bird, away from the place where you failed or were hurt. But for the noble one this is about more than just self-preservation: he still has a light to carry and care for, and a direction to go. Adversity will not make him give up; he is focused single-mindedly on his purpose.

It's best to start such a journey alone, without stopping to join with others and blend your thinking with theirs. You travel more lightly if you don't take other people's ideas on board.

Those who preside over this space and govern its culture will naturally have something to say about a purpose so different from theirs. Your life would certainly be easier if you could have their support – but in its absence, you will safeguard your light by carrying it away.

Line 2   *'Brightness hidden, wounded in the left thigh.*
For rescue, use the power of a horse.
Good fortune.'

You have received a serious injury that threatens to immobilize you, and it seems you are alone and without help. To be saved from this plight and get yourself moving again, you will need to draw on a greater strength and spirit.

Your horse may arise within you, or it may come galloping to the rescue from outside. The important thing is how freely and powerfully it moves. This is the energy you need to carry yourself forward into new places: grasp it and harness it.

Line 3 *'Brightness hidden, hunting in the south.*
Gets their great leader.
Afflicted constancy is not possible.'

Wounded and in darkness, you decide to do more than just hide away; you set out on an active, determined hunt for what oppresses the light. And you have success! You grasp the source of the problem and the key to its solution.

However, this is not the same as already having a *completed* solution. You have an insight of enduring value; for this to be realized, for the light to return, will take time and constancy.

If you rush to make the light fully manifest, you risk further injury. You need to carry your understanding through with a steadfast determination; you simply cannot do this if you are still motivated by the experience of injury, and feverishly anxious to have everything safely resolved.

Line 4 *'Entering into the left belly,*
Catching the heart of brightness hidden.
And going out through the gate from the courtyard.'

It is not enough to think things out rationally. The belly is the home of emotions, sympathies and 'gut feelings', and this is your way in to the heart of the matter.

There, you can sense what wounds and oppresses the light; you can feel the nature of the light itself, and your own heart's intention. The firmest, most unshakeable sense of what you are called to do comes from entering into the darkness.

But it's not good to linger, isolated, in those claustrophobic emotional depths. Bring the understanding you gained there back out into the world, look at it in new ways and fresh contexts, and move towards a place where you can act on it.

Line 5 *'Prince Ji's brightness hidden.*
Constancy bears fruit.'

This is Prince Ji's line. He stays loyal to his light and keeps it hidden: he understands that being clear is not the same as shining out. In secret, he is already living in accordance with truth.

Moreover, constancy is bearing fruit. There *will* come a time when the inner light can be manifest in the outside world. Meanwhile, it is important not to be discouraged by how little power you appear to have: real value and strength have nothing whatsoever to do with these appearances.

Line 6 *'Not bright, dark.*
At first rises up to heaven,
Later enters into the earth.'

The sun rises high in the sky, and then at night it enters into the earth. Light and dark are balanced in the natural cycle, and neither lasts forever, so why be afraid of the dark?

And from this perspective, you can also see that everything in your life must contain darkness as well as light, and you cannot build anything of pure light without clay. Let your aspirations rise to heaven and shine out brightly, but also enter deeply into the ordinary earth your experience grows from.

Hexagram 37, *People in the Home*

Key Questions

Where are the boundaries of the 'home' you inhabit?
How are you building inner and outer relationships into a home?
What kinds of growth does this environment support?

Oracle

'People in the home.
A woman's constancy is fruitful.'

The old Chinese character for 'home' shows a pig under a roof. A home is where people rear a pig together, sharing wealth, work and value. People in the home cooperate in their shared space and invest in it together (as in a family, workplace, school of thought or culture), and within the structure it provides they can recognize and understand what is valuable.

To create a successful home, you need to have the constancy of a woman. Steadily, over time, your work creates a space in which all can grow freely into their natural form, and find their place and their connections with others. You allow space for new things to enter and grow, becoming part of the whole inner ecosystem. You keep the space for living in.

Image

'Wind comes forth originally from fire: People in the Home.
A noble one's words have substance and her actions are
consistent.'

A strong fire in the hearth will create its own draught – the light and warmth at the centre of the home translating into far-reaching influence in the world. It represents a constant, living awareness that pervades the structure and makes its presence felt in everything the noble one says and does.

Also, the fire needs a free flow of air to burn cleanly and steadily. Real words and consistent actions keep it alight.

Sequence

People in the Home follows from Hexagram 36, Brightness Hidden:

'Injury on the outside naturally means turning back towards the home, and so People in the Home follows.'

The home is a refuge. Inner light that had to be hidden away from the outside world is secure here, and finds expression. When you are unappreciated or unseen, you turn back and connect with like-minded people.

Pair

People in the Home forms a pair with Hexagram 38, Opposing:

'Opposing means outside. People in the Home means inside.'

These two hexagrams describe a single landscape: every inside must have its outside. Inside, you find your fellows, those who share your vision. Outside are the foreigners, who see differently and do not belong in this home.

CHANGING LINES

Line 1 *'With barriers, there is a home.*
Regrets vanish.'

When you start to mark out the plot, when you build walls to separate the inside from the outside, you are founding a home. Then with internal partitions to give each person their place, relationships within the space will be settled harmoniously. The new walls interrupt old patterns of behaviour and protect against old injuries and fears, and so regrets vanish; a new home is also a fresh start.

Without the barriers, we felt insecure and unsure of our places; our space was unprotected against what did not belong there; its boundaries were unclear and constantly renegotiated. Once the walls are built, we feel intact; secure in our own identity, we are much better placed to relate well to other people. These are good foundations for a lifetime of organic growth and evolution.

Line 2 *'No direction to pursue,*
Stay in the centre and cook.
Constancy, good fortune.'

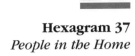
This is a time to concentrate on people's immediate needs, not distant aspirations or grand plans. All the necessary ingredients are already in your home, so there's no call for you go out in pursuit of more. You may find that the centre is connected to everywhere else.

The work you do here might seem to be nothing more than a daily round of chores – but in fact, over time, you are steadily cultivating a space fit to receive great things. When food is prepared in the centre with care and attention, people and spirits may come to share in it.

Line 3 *'People in the home scold and scold,*
Regrets, danger: good fortune.
Wife and child giggle and giggle.
In the end, shame.'

An influx of energy intensifies emotions, challenges the established ways and puts the relationships in the home to the test. There is no perfect response to this, but the better option is to claim responsibility for the order of your space, if need be by arguing out how things will work. This will be painful and dangerous, but it leads to clarification. Better that than to forfeit the woman's constancy.

The wife is meant to be the one who creates the home, as a safe context for real, grounded relationships. But here, she is giggling with the children, shying away from her power and responsibility. This means that when you need to be home-making and housekeeping (that is, taking charge of resources), you only 'play house', with fantasy taking the place of explicit agreement. At first, this is very pleasant and comfortable, but there is shame in the end: nothing changes, and neither thinking nor communication gets any clearer.

Line 4 *'Enriching the home – great good fortune.'*
Riches are stored up in the home; it is good to invest more there.

What enriches the home? Harmony, sound friendship, and a wealth of exchange between people.

Line 5 *'The king enters his own home.*
Do not worry. Good fortune.'

The king has the power of decision; he cannot be coerced. It is his free choice to enter into relationship; when he does so, he takes charge of his space and is responsible for who and what may enter it. With the king in his home, there is no uncertainty, no need for worry; outer relationships will be a true image of inner ones.

Line 6 *'With truth and confidence like authority.*
In the end, good fortune.'

The influence of the home is beginning to radiate beyond its walls. It gives you a place to stand and be present, where you can wield your truth powerfully and make a strong impression. As the Image says, the noble one's words have substance and her actions are consistent.

Such influence will take time and consistent work, and it's as well not to fall into over-confidence, but you can make your true presence felt. You are moving on from the home; where will you go?

Hexagram 38, *Opposing*

What if the difference were not a threat?
How could this tension be creative?
If you can't see eye to eye, what *can* you see?

Oracle

'Opposing.
Small affairs, good fortune.'

'Opposing' describes irreducible differences – desires, motivations and especially ways of seeing that diverge from one another. 'Opposing' people see *differently* even when they're looking at the same scene; they are utterly strange to each other, as if they came from different planets.

With an inner state of 'Opposing', you contain mutually contradictory impulses – like two siblings under one roof – or see from two angles at once. You might see things not only for what they are, but also for what they mean, as if they were omens.

In small affairs, this kind of difference of view means good fortune. It's a challenge, a source of comedy, or a creative stimulus. In matters of great personal importance, though, where people's sense of identity is threatened by a different way of seeing, it will stir up survival instincts and trigger conflict. If you can scale matters down to 'small affairs', it becomes much easier to give space to both visions.

Image

'Fire above, lake below: Opposing.
A noble one both harmonizes and separates.'

The elements of this situation are fire and water. You can't blend them together into a compromise. But kept safely apart, they create harmony: the sun sparkles on the lake; the light of awareness shines on the inner currents of emotion. A noble one lives with opposition, simply by understanding what harmonizes and what is to be held apart.

Sequence

Opposing follows from Hexagram 37, People in the Home:

'When the way of the home is exhausted, you naturally turn away, and so Opposing follows.'

There comes a point when you can no longer find yourself as part of a group; you want to assert your separate identity, or explore something new, outside the safe and familiar walls.

CHANGING LINES

Line 1   *'Regrets vanish.*
          Lost horse: don't pursue it, it returns of itself.
          See hateful people - no mistake.'

This is the first encounter with opposition, inner or outer. Your horse runs away from you – and the horse represents something immensely precious, sometimes your own strength to move forward confidently and with purpose. People appear hateful, as if they were the horse thieves.

How are you to respond to this? Are there actions to be taken, commitments to be made?

Your first impulse might be to mourn the loss, hate the people, and go running after the horse to drag it back to its stable. But you can't catch a fleeing horse like this; you'll only frighten it further away. If you let it, the horse will eventually return on its own, and regrets will vanish.

As for the hateful – or hate-filled – people, there is no mistake if you only see them. There's no need to react at all.

Line 2   *'Meeting a master in the lane - not a mistake.'*

Outside the home, far beyond the walls, you meet a master: a helper and guide. The lane is a neutral, outside space, not part of your home. So a meeting here need not be about creating a long-term relationship, and it need not be planned. It's better not to try to make it fit within rules and expectations.

Even though you may not feel particularly comfortable out here, the encounter is not a mistake. It can be a very direct way to receive a message about something you need to see.

Line 3   *'Seeing the cart dragged back, the oxen stopped*
          Your men branded and their noses cut off,
          With no beginning, there is an end.'

As you embark on your journey, you have a very unpleasant insight into what to expect out on the road. Being full of ideals and rich in resources is no protection – if anything, it only increases the friction between you and everything else until you're dragged to a humiliating halt. You see daunting visions of your vulnerability to attack and disgrace.

And yet, even though your plans are frustrated and your start could hardly be less promising, there will still be an end. There may be no visible way, yet something still brings you through to a resolution.

Line 4 *'Opposed, alone.*
Meet an inspiring man.
Joining together in truth and confidence.
Danger, no mistake.'

On the outside, lonely and isolated as an orphan, you meet an inspiration. Joining and interacting freely gives you an experience of presence, unanimity and fearless trust – the very opposite of 'opposing'.

If you are aware of how vulnerable your isolation has made you, you can recognize the danger here: what are you giving up for this 'joining together'? Yet the creative energy of the connection is real; what is dangerous is not necessarily a mistake.

Line 5 *'Regrets vanish.*
Your ancestor bites through the skin.
Why would going on be wrong?'

The gulf of opposition is decisively overcome; the differences are bitten through; regrets vanish. It's as if you had prepared a meal, and the ancestral spirits honoured you by attending. Their presence is not gentle or comfortable, but it is full of power.

You reconnect – perhaps with another person, or with the creative energy that comes from your roots and your original purpose. Instead of regretting the past, you find strength there, and good reasons to move forward on your path.

Line 6 *'Opposed, alone.*
Seeing pigs covered in muck,
The chariot loaded with devils.
At first drawing the bow,
Then relaxing the bow.
Not robbers at all, but matrimonial allies.
Going on meets the rain, and so there is good fortune.'

Isolated and alone as an orphan, you are acutely aware of how easily you could be hurt. You see nightmare visions; everything seems to be just another omen of ugliness and fear; there is an all-consuming mistrust. You draw your bow to defend yourself against all comers.

But then you look again, and relax the bow, recognizing that what seemed to be coming to steal from you actually comes to bless and enrich you. Now on your journey you meet rain: releasing tension, and promising good crops. What is different is not necessarily your enemy; it could be your partner. Opposition becomes the source of expansion, fertility and growth; the home is enriched as its boundaries are redrawn.

Hexagram 39, *Limping*

Key Questions

Where can you find help?
How could you see the obstacles differently?
Can you imagine going a different way?

Oracle

'Limping. Fruitful in the southwest,
Not fruitful in the northeast.
Fruitful to see great people.
Constancy, good fortune.'

When life has become an uphill struggle, it's wise to fall back to the southwest. The 'southwest' represents a realm of friendly allies and sun-warmed fields; the 'northeast' is dark and mountainous, the way of calling and adventure.

So this is a time to take a step back from the struggle and connect with people more than with ideals. (Even if the responsibility is yours alone, the work need not be.) Really facing a problem means being prepared to tackle it in a different way, not just trudging doggedly onwards until the path peters out beneath your feet.

Seeing great people helps you to keep travelling towards your long-term vision despite the obstacles and course corrections. You may literally find a 'great person' with the experience and wisdom to reorient you; you may be guided by an inner vision of human potential.

Yu the Great, the hero who conquered the floods, toiled for years to build dykes and dredge rivers, and was left with a limp. But he succeeded in the end because of what he did differently: enlisting the help of people and spirits, and honouring the flow of the water.

Image

'Above the mountain, there is water: Limping.
A noble one turns himself around to renew his character.'

The path ahead is hard and dangerous, and it is time to find another way. The clouds that rise above the mountain become the stream flowing down it. It changes course lightly and easily, naturally finding a path of least resistance, always in motion.

Embodying the qualities of mountain and stream, the noble one will join the firmness of his inner resolve with fluid commitment, renewing his strength of character by turning his whole self around.

Sequence

From Hexagram 38, Opposition:

'Turning away naturally means hardship, and so Limping follows.'

When you are alienated from others, life is hard. Nothing is provided for you; everything comes only by your own effort; you struggle, and it is time to look southwest.

Pair

Limping forms a pair with Release, Hexagram 40:

'Release means letting things take their time; Limping means hardship.'

Release is a time of flow; this is a time of struggle. Release is free to follow a chosen path; Limping is unavoidably handicapped and obstructed. And yet… Limping is also the time for 'turning your self around' and finding another way – and that contains the potential for release.

CHANGING LINES

Line 1 *'Going on, limping; coming back, praise.'*

This path you have set out on is proving difficult, maybe impassable. Carrying on as before will only be more and more of a struggle, so it's no bad thing to pause here and rethink your chosen route. Turn towards encouragement and recognition; anticipate better things to come. Look to future achievement for your inspiration, not to precedent, and raise your sights.

Line 2 *'A king, a servant: limping and limping.*
In no way is he himself the cause.'

A time of intense, ongoing difficulties. Yet this experience of 'limping and limping' doesn't necessarily tell you anything about its cause. Things go wrong for you, not because of who you are, but because

of what or whom you serve, the role you play or the position you fill.

The 'king' could be simply your work, or your chosen allegiance – or something that chose you, as Yu was chosen to struggle against the floods. In any case, what you are experiencing as the problem stems from this deeper cause; it may be part of some bigger, unfolding story of which you're quite unaware. There could be an opening here into that story, a chance to reach the deeper truth below the surface. Or it might just be a chance to put your difficulties in perspective, knowing they're not all about you.

Line 3 *'Going on, limping; coming back, turnaround.'*

The connection and belonging you seek is not to be found along this path. The more you press on, the harder it gets. So pause in your striving and rethink… beyond all this struggle, where do you ultimately belong? Imagine what you could create if you turned yourself around to follow those natural affinities and renewed your energies through a complete change of direction.

Line 4 *'Going on, limping; coming back, connection.'*

This situation exerts a powerful 'pull' on you, maybe in a couple of directions at once. It's natural to focus in on deciding how you can handle it. But pause and reconsider – and not only your personal direction, role and feelings. Maybe you, as one vulnerable individual, *can't* handle this. But in broadening your perspective, you rediscover how you are part of a larger whole. That might mean making an authentic, practical connection with a supportive group that's adequate to the task.

Line 5 *'Greatly limping; partners come.'*

Yu the Great was called by heaven to conquer the floods through long, hard toil. Because of the clarity of his calling, and the quality of his character, he could gather to him all the help he needed.

When things are hardest, help will come. When you envisage a life on the other side of these struggles, and dedicate yourself to reaching it, you will attract people and energies ready to invest themselves in the same work. The important thing is to complete the work – to get through the hard times, to overcome the floods. Have the humility to see that you need help, and to recognize and claim it when it comes.

Line 6 *'Going on, limping; coming back, mastery.*
Good fortune. Fruitful to see a great person.'

You don't have to keep battling on as before. There is so much more to be gained – in maturity and in solid personal achievement – by coming back. This doesn't mean you give up and stop, and nor does it mean instantly escaping the struggle. When you come back, you join and interact with the *whole* of the situation, embracing all of its potential and becoming part of its greater evolution.

A 'great person' lives on a larger scale and sees a broader perspective, above and beyond this time of struggle into whole other dimensions of growth. When you see a great person – whether in your inner or outer worlds – you share their vision.

Hexagram 40, *Release*

Key Questions

If nothing could bind you, where would you go?
Do you 'have to'? Who says?
Which path leads to where you want to be?

Oracle

'Release. Fruitful in the southwest.
With no place to go,
To turn round and come back is good fortune.
With a direction to go,
Daybreak, good fortune.'

To 'release' is to liberate, to solve problems, to untie knots. The first step towards release is a move 'southwest': no longer battling on to pursue the mission, but going back to your roots and reconnecting with home and allies. When you know where you're coming from, it becomes a lot easier to be clear about where you're going.

If your path has no real destination, turn back; if it has purpose, start your journey as early as you can. If you have no good reason to continue on as before, come back to your starting point and let that cycle reach its end; if you have a goal in mind, why not start exploring ways to attain it right away?

This would be such simple advice, if only we didn't spend our lives being 'pulled' down paths that lead nowhere, as if by invisible strings.

Image

'Thunder and rain do their work: Release.
A noble one pardons transgressions and
forgives crimes.'

Imagine the air after a thunderstorm: clean, clear, all the tension released. Humans do the work of thunder and rain through forgiveness. Just as, in the trigrams, thunder comes forth from an inner trigram

representing rain and flowing water, so action can spring from fluidity rather than from a rigid stance. (Think of a master of Tai Ji in motion, or a springing cat.)

Forgiveness frees us from the bonds of inevitability: a line crossed need not mean there *must* be retribution; punishment doesn't have to follow from crime. It's rare that we're truly 'forced' to respond in a certain way, or 'obliged' to make up for our own past mistakes or omissions.

Sequence

Release follows from Hexagram 39, Limping:

'Things cannot end with hardship, and so Release follows. Release means letting things take their time.'

There comes a time when there has been enough struggle. Release means ending the battle with the world and starting to reconnect with its natural flow.

CHANGING LINES

Line 1 *'No mistake.'*
The simplest, most fundamental beginning to Release: this is not wrong, and there is no blame to attribute.

Even if you find yourself in a weaker position, vulnerable to other people's decisions, there is no mistake. You can only do what you can. It might even be a release to see how you are not responsible for everything that happens around you.

Line 2 *'In the field, taking three foxes.*
Gaining a golden arrow.
Constancy, good fortune.'
These foxes are wily creatures with powers of elusiveness and disguise. They create fantasy and deluded imaginings; they are not what they seem. But now they are exposed, out in the field. This is your chance to differentiate between fantasy and reality and take their power away.

You gain a golden arrow, emblem of your newly liberated power to fly straight and true to what you need. The constancy of an arrow in flight means good fortune.

Line 3 *'Shouldering a burden while also riding in a carriage*
Invites the arrival of bandits.
Constancy, shame.'

Either you carry the burden, or else you are carried along. Either the weight is yours alone to bear, or else you have gifts and support that allow you to travel further and more freely.

But to attempt both at once only goes to show that you haven't mastered the nature of carriages, and are unsuited to ride in one. 'Bandits' are magnetically drawn to such disharmony: other people ready to take what you never really owned, or your own inner thieves of self-confidence and purpose.

Trying to hold on to two incompatible roles is no longer sustainable; carrying on in this inauthentic state leads to shame. This is the moment to ask yourself what is natural and sustainable for you. Are you comfortable 'riding in the carriage' – is this who you are, or would you be more comfortable with a slower, more down-to-earth approach? Is this baggage yours to carry, or would you still be yourself if you relinquished your grip on it?

Line 4 *'Releasing the thumbs also.*
Partners arrive, hence truth and confidence.'

When you release your thumbs, you release your grip. Instead of holding on to how things 'ought' to work out, you open your hands and invite a more spontaneous connection with people and forces you can trust to help you. When you let go your requirements for how things (especially relationships) must be, you release the situation's latent potential; you can even attain what you sought quite naturally and easily.

Line 5 *'A noble one, bound, is released.*
Good fortune.
There is truth towards small people.'

The noble one is not truly trapped: she can find a way to express herself even within constraints, because they never touch her essential self. Simply by being who she is, regardless of opinions or circumstances, her presence communicates freely and powerfully with others. She can reach and convince even those who lack that quality of imaginative freedom, and restore sincerity even where people are hidebound by rules and roles.

Line 6 *'A prince uses this to shoot a hawk, on the top of the high ramparts.*
He gets it. Nothing that does not bear fruit.'

Shooting the hawk releases the tension in the bowstring; dealing directly with something ominous that looms over you (or you and your people) releases the tension in the situation and puts it to good use. It shows clear vision and unwavering focus.

First you wait, keyed up and uncertain, for the moment to act, knowing you'll only get one shot at this. Then everything lines up perfectly, and you know you can do it.

Hexagram 41, *Decreasing*

Key Questions

Why do you want to make such an offering?
How much is truly asked of you?
Could this be simpler?

Oracle

'Decreasing: there is truth and confidence.
From the source, good fortune.
Not a mistake, there can be constancy.
Fruitful to have a direction to go.
How to use this?
Two simple baskets may be used for the offering.'

The early Chinese character for 'Decreasing' shows a hand with a vessel: decreasing, you pour out what you have in offering. You focus your faith and hope on something higher than your everyday life, and sacrifice lower things to this. When you do so with an undivided heart, it opens the flow of good fortune, and your life becomes lighter and simpler.

Yi offers reassurance: even when you have little to give, making offerings is not wrong. Trusting your insight and persevering in your chosen direction, you understand *why* you are doing this, rather than dwelling on what you are giving up. You may still wonder how you can do it, or how much you are expected to give. But the offering need only be modest – not hundreds of animals, but just two baskets. You are not asked to give beyond your means.

Image

'Below the mountain is the lake: Decreasing.
A noble one curbs anger and restrains desires.'

A noble one, when he gives things up, is not without anger and desires: he just keeps them under control, solid as the mountain that contains the lake and limits the flow of its waters.

Without the evaporating waters, the mountainside would be barren; without the mountain, the water would dissipate and be lost. Together, they create a complete landscape: emotions sustaining growth in higher experience, and control deepening your emotional capacity.

Sequence

Decreasing follows from Hexagram 40, Release:

'Letting things take their time naturally means letting go, and so Decreasing follows.'

To release ties and bonds and relinquish control is also a loss – one that makes life simpler.

Pair

Decreasing forms a pair with Hexagram 42, Increasing:

'Decreasing, Increasing: the beginnings of abundance and decline.'

They belong together in a natural cycle – a free flow of giving and receiving, like breathing. To create space for new blessings, you need to empty things out.

CHANGING LINES

Line 1 *'Bringing your own business to an end, going swiftly - not a mistake.*
Considering decreasing it.'

You have many things to do, control and be busy about. You can safely bring them all to an end and move on without delay, thinking instead about what you have to offer.

You need to allow yourself time to learn how to give, and to manage your giving, instead of filling every moment with 'things to do'. Think of ways to be less involved in your business, and hence more available. Be mindful of your connections and commitments, and how giving in one place means taking away from somewhere else. How much you give is not important – what matters is *how* you give, and whether your purpose is aligned with the purpose of those you are giving to.

Line 2 *'Constancy bears fruit,*
Setting out to bring order: pitfall.
Not decreasing, increasing it.'

If you hold fast to the course you have set, this will be fruitful; the need to make everything right at once is a distraction. This is no time to fix things, or people: that would be a huge, futile sacrifice, driven by a hunger for guaranteed security, but only draining your resources. Don't give up your equilibrium in this

way; make your offering smaller and simpler. You may find that your real nourishment does not come from external conditions, and that all can be increased without any great sacrifice on your part.

Line 3 *'Three people walking, hence decreased by one person.*
One person walking, hence gains a friend.'

We naturally go in twos. A group of three is not stable and will decrease to two; one alone will find a companion. So if you want to create a meaningful connection, leave your group, and do not bring a third element – a person, or a preoccupation – with you into a partnership.

It's not easy to sacrifice the security of the group and travel into new places, alone and self-reliant. But this is an offering worth making: in taking the initiative and walking alone, you attract a more authentic relationship, and open up the possibility of being of greater service.

Line 4 *'Decreasing your affliction,*
Sending the message swiftly brings rejoicing – not a mistake.'

Anxiety, alienation from others, or feeling inwardly divided … these things can also be decreased and offered up. Instead of fretting over what to do, take a first step: communicate what you have in mind. However your message may be received, sending it still lessens distance and division. You are choosing a single path, and can no longer keep your options open – but this at least resolves the tension of being in two minds. The message re-establishes inner connection and communication first of all.

Line 5 *'Maybe increased by ten paired tortoise shells,*
Nothing is capable of going against this.
From the source, good fortune.'

An ancient method of divination was to apply heat to tortoise shells and read the patterns of cracks, using the shells in pairs to ask whether or not to do something. Here, a course of action could be unanimously blessed by ten pairs of readings. There is a true and open connection with the spirits, who respond in absolute accord. This is an overwhelming assent; nothing could possibly have the authority to oppose it.

Your good fortune is not as dependent on other factors as you might imagine. No obstacles can impede it; no problems you may have in mind can truly limit it. Take this as your starting point.

Line 6 *'Not decreasing, increasing it – not a mistake.*
Constancy, good fortune.
Fruitful to have a direction to go.
Gaining servants, not a home.'

What you offer up here brings blessing and is no real loss, because you are following a good course; you do well to persevere. Rather than stopping at what you have gained, as if it were your goal, keep looking through and beyond it, asking where it takes you next, how it is developing, and how it can be of service.

The reward for your offering is not a place to settle down; it does not define where you go or what you do. Instead, you gain the support and strength to move in your chosen direction. There is no intrinsic value in this; the value all lies in what you are going to do with it.

Hexagram 42, *Increasing*

Key Questions

What would you do if you knew you were blessed?
What if there were no limits?
What could change for the better?

Oracle

 *'Increasing, fruitful to have a direction to go.
Fruitful to cross the great river.'*

The old Chinese character for Increasing shows a pot filled to overflowing. It means blessing and superabundance, like the timely rain that brings a rich harvest.

Increase simply *flows*, without limit; there is no need for restrictive frameworks to contain it, but only for tools to work with it. When you are blessed, it is good to respond with purpose and movement: participating in the increase, pouring more in, you receive more in return. Let yourself imagine where you want to be, and take the first steps that commit you to going there. This is how to keep the momentum.

Image

*'Wind and thunder: Increasing.
A noble one sees improvement, and so she changes.
When there is excess, she corrects it.'*

Wind and thunder are agents of change. Thunder is like the inner spark of initiative and will; wind is a far-reaching influence in the world, free-moving because of its endless ability to shape itself to the terrain. So the noble one moves as decisively as thunder and with the versatility of the wind; she does not hold fast to a chosen direction, but responds to whatever opportunities for improvement she can see.

Sequence

Increasing follows from Hexagram 41, Decreasing:

'Decreasing and not reaching an end must mean Increasing.'

Decrease is the offering, emptying out the vessel; increase is the blessing, the pot filled to overflowing. There is the willingness to have less and make things simpler, and the willingness to receive more and become richer. Each phase leads into the other, moving in a cycle.

CHANGING LINES

Line 1 *'Fruitful to use this to make great beginnings.*
From the source, good fortune, no mistake.'

Use your blessings! This is the moment to get underway, and make the greatest possible use of your gifts. There's no need to limit yourself to modest, sensible, short-term goals: allow yourself an unhampered view of all the possibilities. Although this is just the starting point, perhaps you can see the emerging shape of the full, finished work. Embrace the energy, and act.

Line 2 *'Maybe increased by ten paired tortoise shells.*
Nothing is capable of going against this.
Ever-flowing constancy, good fortune.
The king uses this to make offerings to the supreme being: good fortune.'

This refers to an ancient oracle, read from the cracks in heated tortoise shells. These readings were made in pairs to verify whether or not to undertake something; now, the oracle would agree, not once but ten times. The channel to the spirits is open; the response is clear and true. Nothing – no doubts, confusions or 'bad signs' – can ever overrule such a confirmation.

You have a blessing of unshakeable intrinsic value. It is good to respond with a fluid steadfastness: to stay with it, and invest your whole, true self, but also to stay mobile and responsive to change. Receive your blessing as a king, who understands he is blessed, and chooses to dedicate the whole changing experience to a higher good.

Line 3 *'Increased by means of disaster work,*
Not a mistake.
With truth and confidence, moving to the centre,
Notify the prince using a jade baton.'

When something disastrous happens, there is work to be done – and you do have the means and capacity to act. You can take your place with confidence and assume your full measure of responsibility.

The first step will be to talk with people who can help you, conveying your willingness to work together with them in trust. Your clear intent and resolve are your credentials: experiencing harsh times gives you an authority as pure and tough as jade.

Line 4
'Moving to the centre,
Notify the prince, he follows.
Fruitful to use this to inspire trust in moving the city.'

Moving freely with the flow of increase, you go to the centre of things and become actively involved in its changes. It's time for the city to be transplanted to a more auspicious site. Rather than making do with how things are, people must disengage completely from their old, ill-omened situation and move into a more harmonious alignment with heaven.

Clear communication is essential to secure agreement – both inner and outer – for such a radical shift. You will need to enlist the leader's cooperation, and earn the trust and consent of all involved.

Line 5
'True and confident, with a benevolent heart,
No question: good fortune from the source.
Truth, confidence and benevolence are my own strength.'

This is the heart of Increasing and blessing. When you are completely present to the flow of nourishing energy, when what you send out into the world is free, true and generous, then there is nothing more you need ask. It is safe to give; you can trust that what you send out is the source of what returns to you.

This has the power to re-create the whole circulation that sustains you. Truth and benevolence are the living essence of who you are.

Line 6
'Absolutely no increase in this,
Maybe someone strikes this one.
The heart's foundation is not lasting.
Pitfall.'

Desire and intention are at their peak, yet increase is not flowing at all. Fluid responsiveness has gone too far, and tipped over into opportunism – a desire to explore all possibilities and follow impulse, or just the line of least resistance. There is no will to persevere, to commit to a single direction and hold to it consistently through change.

If you are only interested in what you need to receive, and not in giving, you will not invest yourself reliably in relationships or create real connections. You are likely to attract hostility and misfortune, and let yourself and other people down.

Hexagram 43, *Deciding*

Key Questions

What do you stand for?
How do you define yourself?
What belongs in your realm, and where do you
need to make a clean break?

Oracle

'Deciding, tell it in the king's chambers.
With truth, call out, there is danger.
Notify your own city.
Fruitless to take up arms;
Fruitful to have a direction to go.'

The old Chinese character for 'Deciding' shows a hand holding up a token – asserting your
identity and right to be heard, even in the king's chambers. This is where decision begins, at the
very centre of power. That centre might be inside your own mind, and yet still not feel safe.
Declaring the truth loud and clear is dangerous; it stirs up old ghosts, inner and outer. Yet better
this than ignoring and neglecting them.

As the message of the decision spreads out from the centre, it is fruitless to take up arms:
this is a time to communicate, not fight. It will serve you better to focus with clear intention on
what you're moving towards, rather than what you're reacting against.

Image

'Lake above heaven: Deciding.
A noble one distributes riches to reach those below,
She dwells in power and virtue, and also shuns things.'

A lake above heaven is a cloud: sharing the blessing of rain, and always pure, never in contact
with the mud. The noble one's generosity is like this: a pure, inspired expression of her character,
without ulterior motive. She gives, and also knows what to stay away from.

Sequence

Deciding follows from Hexagram 42, Increasing:

'Increasing and not reaching an end must mean breakthrough, and so Deciding follows. Deciding means breaking through.'

As more and more is poured in, the limits must surely break. Instead of travelling with the cycle from increase to decrease, you take a positive decision to use and share the blessing.

Pair

Deciding forms a pair with Hexagram 44, Coupling:

'Coupling means meeting, supple meets firm.'
'Deciding means breaking up, firm breaks up supple.'

Hexagram 43 has five firm, unbroken lines pushing out a single supple, open line. They embody an assertion of identity that breaks through indecision. In Hexagram 44, the single open line finds its way back.

CHANGING LINES

Line 1 *'Vigour in the leading foot.*
Going on without control means making mistakes.'
You're eager to cross the line and prove yourself, and bring about much-needed change. However, this doesn't mean you can sustain the journey your feet are itching to take. Your desire to get underway needs to be matched by a broader awareness of where you're going.

Line 2 *'Alarmed, calling out.*
Evening and night, bearing arms
Do not fear.'
Now the call to change has come, it's more important than ever to carry your message or charge well – yet impossible to know what the change may bring. So you are far from confident about responding to the call, and peer out into the dark, constantly on guard against all possible threats. But because you are alert, you need not be afraid.

Line 3 *'Vigour in the cheekbones means a pitfall.*
Noble one decides, decides.
Goes on alone, meets the rain,
And is indignant as if she were soaked through.
Not a mistake.'

You could locate your power in your cheekbones: you could be hard, rigidly unresponsive, concentrating on the face you present to others. This would repel relationships and lead to misfortune.

Or you could decide like the noble one, who takes a stand as herself without wearing a mask of strength. Such supple authenticity opens the way for real exchange with real people: full, free, enriching – and messy: your dignity may not survive. But the rain makes things grow.

Line 4 *'Thighs without flesh,*
Moving awkwardly now.
Lead a sheep on a rope, regrets vanish.
Hear words, not trusted.'

Taking a decision doesn't immediately make life easier. For Yu the Great, it meant accepting the responsibility to overcome the great floods and create safe, dry land to feed the people. Moved by a restless desire to accomplish his task, he travelled and laboured constantly, so that his thighs wasted away.

Such long-term decisions become credible when they are made in actions, not words. Rather than talking about it, it's better simply to let your actions speak, like the man who leads out a sheep to show his surrender. Regrets vanish when, instead of fighting the present reality, you go to meet it with acceptance. This truly demonstrates resolve.

Line 5 *'Amaranth on high ground.*
Decide, decide.
Move to the centre, no mistake.'

The nutritious, healing amaranth grows on the high ground by itself; nobody planted it there. Although you didn't intend or design it, there is something of value available – but not within easy reach. Is it worthwhile to go after it? You are well placed to decide how best to use your energy. What would be the balanced action?

Line 6 *'Not calling out.*
In the end, pitfall.'

The Oracle speaks of 'calling out with truth'. If truth goes unspoken – perhaps out of fear, or a desire to keep it in a pure state of potential, or a conviction of self-sufficiency – then there will be misfortune in the end.

Hexagram 44, *Coupling*

Key Questions

What would be an adequate response to this new energy?
How far could this change go?
How far will you let it go?

Oracle

'Coupling, the woman is powerful.
Do not take this woman.'

'Coupling' means meeting, and also a woman who gives birth to the heir – the powerful woman. She represents someone (of either sex) or something with a profound and mysterious power to attract you, to take over, and to change everything. She moves you, re-energizes and gives birth to new life.

   The oracle warns you not to take the woman – not to try to seize control of her, and not to marry her. Do not imagine that you can bring her under control, assimilate her into your life and continue as before. Such a marriage cannot last.

   This woman has more power than any system where you might try to contain her. She might bring desires that undermine a well-balanced life, or an irruption of feeling into a realm of abstractions, or chance and irrationality to threaten a logical, ordered mind.

   Perhaps you will stand fast and resist this power's attraction. Perhaps you will embrace her briefly, and let your life be transformed by the encounter. But you cannot take her or marry her.

Image

'Below heaven is the wind: Coupling.
The prince sends out mandates and commands to the four corners of the earth.'

The wind travels everywhere under heaven and penetrates every corner of the world. The prince receives the mandate, orders from heaven, and it penetrates to his core and travels through him. He cannot control or contain such power, but he can broadcast it to change his whole realm.

Sequence

Coupling follows from Hexagram 43, Deciding:

'Breaking through must mean meeting, and so Coupling follows: Coupling means meeting.'

Hexagram 43 broke through indecision and separated cleanly from all that did not belong. Now, whatever you excluded comes back to meet you, and opens a space where unknowable possibilities can enter.

CHANGING LINES

Line 1 *'Held fast by a golden chock. Constancy: good fortune.*
With a direction to go, see the pitfall:
A scrawny pig can be trusted to kick and struggle.'

The restraints that hold you back are important things in their own right. They are like brakes; they give you control over whether or not you move forward, which is a beautiful, valuable thing to have. To stay with this, to persist in exercising control, brings good fortune.

But this is the beginning of Coupling, with all its powers of attraction, and so a restless drive and desire is stirring: you want to be elsewhere. Before you follow this desire, though, step back and see it for what it is. It is certainly strong, but with the strength of a hungry pig, craving food and struggling mindlessly against its tether.

Line 2 *'In this basket there are fish – not a mistake.*
Not fruitful to entertain guests.'

You set your wickerwork trap in the river, and it has caught fish. This is the sign of something promising: a beginning, an idea, an inner conviction, a chance of future growth. It's worth holding on to while you discover where its value lies for you.

What you do *not* have is a guarantee of results. It's far too early to introduce your hope to a wider context and expect it to bear fruit. For now, it should have your inner space to itself, free from premature expectations. You can best care for any long-term possibilities by not presuming on them.

Line 3   'Thighs without flesh,
        Moving awkwardly now.
        Danger, no great mistake.'

Yu the Great was charged by Heaven with the task of conquering the floods, and his thighs wasted away with the decades of hard labour. You are 'coupled' to a demanding task, responsibility or situation. It is awkward, uncomfortable and endlessly hard work; it does not allow you to rest, and you never asked for it. The demands, and your emotional reaction against them, threaten to undermine your equilibrium.

And yet – this is real, authentic work you are doing, and you have the resources for it: however difficult it gets, you can keep moving.

Line 4   'In this basket, no fish. Rising up, pitfall.'

Looking to integrate the new energy into your life, you lower your wickerwork trap into the river. If there are fish, these will be omens of a lasting, fertile relationship. But instead the omen tells you plainly: there is nothing in this for you now. You have no real possibilities to act on, so it would be disastrous to try to start anything.

You have yet to connect with the true nature of the thing (or person); it does not fit into your picture of how things are; it has not swum into your net. Perhaps you need to move your nets, draw a new picture; perhaps you would do better to let this one go: the oracle does not say.

Line 5   'Using willow to wrap melons.
        Containing a thing of beauty,
        It comes falling from its source in heaven.'

What you have here comes falling into your lap 'out of the blue'. It is a beginning to receive and nurture with care, as people would wrap a melon to protect it against bruising as it ripens.

This is the beginning of an incubation period, like a pregnancy, and the final shape of this 'thing of beauty' is still hidden away, growing and transforming – perhaps into a whole new pattern to live by. It may not be anything you had planned for, and you may or may not have a place for it. Much depends on the quality of your availability, and whether you will create space for a relationship with this unexpected, maybe unasked-for gift in its entirety.

Line 6   'Coupling with your horns.
        Shame – not a mistake.'

You meet the incoming energy – the subversive, feminine power described in the Oracle – with lowered horns. You cannot possibly live with this power, and you will go to extremes to prevent it from overturning everything. Perhaps you ward it off as a threat, or lock horns pre-emptively to wrestle it into submission; in either case, you are trying to take back control and ensure any relationship only proceeds on your own terms.

This combative approach might work, but you will emerge with bruises, and feeling that this clash was not a very adequate response. However, it is not wrong to use your horns. Grappling with this power and keeping control is probably the best you can do in the circumstances.

Hexagram 45, *Gathering*

Key Questions

What is asked of you?
What are you investing in?

Oracle

> *'Gathering, creating success.*
> *The king enters his temple.*
> *Fruitful to see great people, creating success.*
> *Constancy bears fruit.*
> *Using great sacrificial animals: good fortune.*
> *Fruitful to have a direction to go.'*

The old character for 'Gathering' shows people gathered like grass, or perhaps gathered to bring in the harvest: they have a shared identity, and invest together for a purpose, looking for what will bear fruit. Sometimes this is an external gathering, sometimes an internal one – collecting yourself and integrating your many roles and strengths, getting yourself together. Many people, roles, energies and issues are concentrated in this single focal point.

The king enters his temple to connect his people with the ancestral spirits. This is a time to strengthen shared roots, and understand mundane daily activities as part of a larger story and identity that gives them meaning.

With this connection made, it is time to see great people. Originally this might have meant consulting with diviners, to ensure your offerings were made in harmony with the time and the spirits. Seeing great people (whether in the flesh or with your inner vision) gives you longer-term guidance to align your efforts with your purpose. Then a steady persistence will bear fruit.

And you are making great efforts – and an act of faith – investing the best you have in this gathering. You need those good, deep roots, and clear-sighted guidance, and you need to know where you are going with it all.

Image

> *'Lake higher than the earth: Gathering.*
> *A noble one sets aside weapons and tools, and warns against the unexpected.'*

The reservoir has high earth banks, its water level higher than your home. You can grow more crops, but if it flooded you would lose everything. Poised between intensity and overload, with so much invested in one place, the noble one takes special care. Inwardly, she is quietly resourceful and prepared for trouble; outwardly, she communicates the need to stay watchful.

Sequence

Gathering follows from Hexagram 44, Coupling:

'They meet one another, then they assemble, and so Gathering follows. Gathering means assembling.'

The gathering expands to encompass everything that meets together. Even the untameable, unpredictable forces of change that arrived in Hexagram 44 are integrated here.

Pair

Gathering forms a pair with Hexagram 46, Pushing Upward:

'Gathering means assembling, Pushing Upward means not coming back.'

Before you can set out single-mindedly towards a chosen goal, you must gather your people and resources. The stronger your purpose, the more you will be willing to invest; the more you invest, the less likely you are to turn back. Investment and aspiration are two sides of a single coin.

CHANGING LINES

Line 1 *'There is truth and confidence, but no completion.*
Then confusion, then gathering.
Like a call, one clasp of the hands brings laughter.
Do not worry. Going on, no mistake.'

You have emotional presence, openness and trust between people. What you are missing is a settled relationship you can depend on to safeguard the connection, and a sense of where this is going. This intense confusion of free-floating emotions opens the way for gathering.

All the confusion is resolved and tension released when people simply call out to one another and

clasp hands. No formality is necessary, nor even any words, and you do not need to know how it will work out. Only follow that spontaneous human impulse to reach out and connect, and everything flows from there.

Line 2 *'Being drawn. Good fortune, no mistake.*
With truth and confidence, it is fruitful to make the summer offering.'
Rather than confronting any mistrust directly, you are drawn gradually towards relationship and understanding. It's uncomfortable to be under tension, but it gives you energy and keeps you in motion.

The modest summer offering is made in this forward-looking spirit, anticipating the harvest to come. The quality of your presence and trust is more important than the scale of what you have to offer.

Line 3 *'Now gathering, now lamenting.*
No direction bears fruit.
Going on, no mistake. Small shame.'
The gathering is not harmonious – and because it is charged with such intense emotion, you are acutely vulnerable here. The more you invest yourself, the more painful it gets. This is no longer a purposeful gathering; it's become a drama, with no positive choice you could make that would lead to achievement. So rather than asking loaded questions about where this is going, it is more important just to keep going anyway. The story need not end here. You may feel as if you really ought to be achieving more with this gathering – but hoping for more and making greater efforts is exactly what leads to lamenting.

Line 4 *'Great good fortune, no mistake.'*
You serve a larger objective and are part of a larger gathering, and you understand that you don't have exclusive responsibility for the outcome. It is good to be free to seek your place in this broader landscape; your good fortune lies in your direction, at least as much as in where you find yourself now.

Line 5 *'Gathering, there is a position - no mistake.*
No trust at all.
From the source, ever-flowing constancy - regrets vanish.'
You have your place to stand, your responsibility; you even have the initiative. There is nothing wrong with this, yet it feels insecure and uncertain.

This is the moment to gather your willpower and make a positive choice to be here: you need to *make it yours*. Regrets vanish when you flow into the position like water, filling it without compromising your own essence, and show an enthusiasm that carries conviction.

Line 6 *'Heartfelt lamenting, weeping, snivelling - not a mistake.'*
When all the sacrifices and demands feel like too much, it's natural to express your emotions. The messy extremes of feeling are not wrong, and you do not need anyone's permission to give voice to your sorrow. Break through the blocks to communication; make yourself heard.

Hexagram 46, *Pushing Upward*

Key Questions

Is this something you can commit yourself to?
Where might it take you?
What is the next step?

Oracle

'Pushing upward, creating success from the source.
Make use of seeing great people.
Do not worry.
Set forth to the south, good fortune.'

The old Chinese character for 'Pushing Upward' shows a small ladle used to measure out offerings and official salaries. It suggests a step-by-step ascent, one measure at a time.

This is a vigorous, active time. Come from the source of inspiration and involve it in your work. Make good use of seeing great people, whether in the flesh or with your inner vision, to charge you with the energy to begin your ascent. Use them to inspire you with a vision of possibilities, and for information and help on how to move on upward.

Hard work and steep slopes lie ahead, but the oracle reassures you that you need not worry or doubt. Instead, set your face to the south, as the ruler does: align your initiatives with the natural order (which can be read in the stars and the compass), and set out towards warmth, light and activity.

Image

'Centre of the earth gives birth to wood: Pushing Upward.
A noble one with patient character
Builds up small things to attain the high and great.'

A seed germinates and the plant begins to grow in the centre of the earth. The noble one has the qualities of both the earth and the seedling: flexible, feeling her way upward, small and resilient, and also yielding and nurturing this growth with all the patient power of earth. She understands that

pulling the seedling will not make it grow faster — and so the many small things she achieves will amount to great things in the end.

Sequence

Pushing Upward follows from Hexagram 45, Gathering:

'Assembling and moving higher is called Pushing Upward, and so Pushing Upward follows.'

When people and energies are gathered and have something higher to aim for, then this naturally translates into striving upward. A group of people motivate one another, or an individual 'gathers herself', to muster energy to climb towards the goal.

CHANGING LINES

Line 1 *'Welcomed pushing upward,*
Great good fortune.'
If you push upward, your initiative will be received and welcomed. You will form a connection that supports and encourages all your future efforts. You step into a creative flow, and great things become possible.

Line 2 *'True and confident,*
And so it is fruitful to make the summer offering.
No mistake.'
Your resources are limited (as they are in summer, before the harvest), but it is still good to commit yourself, see what is needed, and offer what you honestly can. It may seem insufficient — not all that you're aiming for — but you can trust that what you have to offer is worth giving. You will at least be moving in the right direction.

More important than the scale of your offering is the authenticity of feeling behind it. This needs to be a wholehearted offering, and one that means something to you.

Line 3 *'Pushing upward in the empty city.'*
This place was once at the centre of the action, full of life and meaning. You might have thought it still would be — or at least, that there would be *something* here to engage with, whether antagonism or welcome — but now it stands empty.

If you are committed to change and progress, it is up to you to move on. Travel straight through towards your objective; do not linger here waiting for the echoes to talk to you.

Line 4 *'The king makes offerings on Mount Qi.*
Good fortune, no mistake.'

Mount Qi was the original sacred mountain of the Zhou people, close to their home. You might make new conquests in remote lands, or you might suffer losses, but the mountain remains, and it sets these things in perspective.

It is time to rededicate yourself to your roots and the source of your strength. Steady your present ambitions by anchoring them to the past. Whether or not you can see any prospect of immediate success, this will ultimately mean good fortune.

Line 5 *'Constancy, good fortune.*
Pushing upward step by step.'

You cannot reach the summit in a single leap. You can only go there step by step, and the only step you can take now is the next one: you cannot miss any out. There is no need to be discouraged by setbacks: when you keep going steadily, you will always be capable of that next step.

Line 6 *'In the dark, pushing upward.*
Fruitful with unceasing constancy.'

The path is hidden from you, there is no map, and your usual ways of navigating are of no use, leaving you confused and vulnerable. This is not a time to change course and explore at random. Instead, constantly and vigilantly check your inner compass and renew your contact with truth. Never stop asking questions.

Hexagram 47, *Confined*

Key Questions

What if you could only rely on yourself?
Who are you, when you are alone?

Oracle

'Confined, creating success.
Constancy of a great person, good fortune.
Not a mistake.
There are words, not trusted.'

The Chinese character for 'Confined' or 'oppressed' shows a tree completely encircled by walls: an image of entrapment and isolation. You are cut off, and cannot reach out to others.

The great person finds good fortune in constancy to an inner ideal. This is the supreme test of character: whether you can hold to your purpose when there is no encouragement, no confirmation from outside, but only your own inner resources. The lack of outward signs of progress does not mean that you are wrong, or that the world is wrong. Rather than resenting the walls, concentrate on the life and growth within them.

Do not place too much value on words: they will not provide you with a way out – neither conversation, nor argument, nor your own reasoning and theorizing. Words alone are only circulating ideas; they lack the real, personal connection that would make them trustworthy.

Image

'Lake without water: Confined.
A noble one carries out the mandate, fulfils her aspiration.'

The lake water has all drained away into the stream below. Where there might have been a sparkling centre of vitality, communication and exchange, there is no water left – no energy for communication.

Even in such straits, a noble one is still active. The lake water drained downward and inward, merging with the stream in a single, strong current. In the same way, a noble one lets her mandate – what she is called on to do – flow together with the aspiration of her own heart. The two strengthen one another and create an inner momentum that follows through to fulfilment.

Sequence

Being Confined follows from Hexagram 46, Pushing Upward:

'Pushing upward and not reaching an end is naturally Confining.'

You drive yourself upward, full of optimism, confidently expecting to reach your goal – and then, *you don't.* And so you find yourself feeling trapped, exhausted by the climb, and also profoundly shaken and betrayed by the way things have failed to work out as they should.

Pair

Confined forms a pair with Hexagram 48, the Well:

'The Well is wholly connected; Confined means meeting together.'

By its nature, the well is already limitlessly connected, while the confined tree must reach down towards the water table. Reaching inward, you find help. Outwardly, the oppressive walls are unbroken – but what might the inner space open onto?

CHANGING LINES

Line 1 *'Buttocks oppressed with a wooden stick,*
Entering into a gloomy valley,
For three years, meeting no-one.'

You feel hurt and maltreated; you are still smarting from the blows. So it is natural to go quiet and back away, and restrict your communication. Perhaps this could be a way to recover some self-assurance. Alternatively, especially if you let it last, it could be a way to plunge yourself into a depressive isolation and waste all the potential joy of relationship.

Line 2 *'Confined while drinking and feasting,*
Scarlet sashes come from all directions.
Fruitful to use thank-offerings and oblations.
Setting out to bring order: pitfall, no mistake.'

You are confined in your ability to share in the give-and-take of relationship, so that even surrounded by people you are still isolated. Messengers in scarlet sashes offer you a meaningful way to participate, and

ask for your response. They represent something important to you – which can complicate the relationship immensely. It's best to respond modestly, with small offerings that gently open the channels of communication. By making gifts only for the sake of giving, you can care for the new connection.

Be cautious about seeking more than this – more responsibility, or more direct control, or more change all at once. If it seems that you are being offered the chance to set your world to rights – however much it may *need* setting to rights – do not take it.

Line 3   *'Confined by stones, grasping at star thistles.*
Entering into his house, does not see his wife. Pitfall.'

Trapped by unyielding circumstances, you reach for help from things that can only hurt you. This is so much more painful than grasping at straws. You must make the transition to a new and stronger support – come home to a safe place – but the real partnership you need is still hidden from you.

Line 4   *'Coming slowly, slowly, confined in a bronze chariot.*
Shame. There is completion.'

A chariot covered in bronze ornamentation is a heavy, lumbering vehicle. It conveys the great importance of the journey (and the traveller), but it is not so swift or agile: it makes it difficult to change direction.

Such an elaborate approach to meeting with people could be embarrassing. It's open to misinterpretation, especially since it makes it so slow and awkward to respond. You yearn for a simpler way to communicate despite the obstacles, and eventually you manage to make the connection.

Line 5   *'Nose cut, feet cut, oppressed by the crimson sashes.*
Then moving slowly brings release.
Fruitful to use offerings and oblations.'

Officials in crimson come to announce a punishment. You can no longer move independently; you lose your own sense of your self and your value. At least, you do if you accept the judgment – but what is the true extent of its power over you? Who is the ruler who invested these officials with such power?

It will take time and thought for you to get free from this. Moving on slowly and gently will ensure you do not escalate the problem or get more heavily involved fighting to change things that will not change. If you cannot act directly on the source of oppression, you can still act on your own inner state, and smooth over the friction in relationships, by using modest offerings.

There are circumstances here you cannot change, but if you are choosing your own response, how could you be trapped?

Line 6   *'Confined by trailing creepers, by unease and discomfort,*
Says, "Acting - regret." With regret, setting forth, good fortune.'

These creepers appear to block your path, but they could be swept aside. There are no real, substantial reasons not to move on. Instead, there is the feeling of being invalidated and isolated; you lose confidence, and then your own anxious imaginings are your greatest restrictions. You feel unhappy where you are, but convince yourself that any action would make things worse. This is not true.

Hexagram 48, *the Well*

Key Questions

What is the ever-present resource you draw from?
What can you do to realize its potential here?

Oracle

 'The Well. Moving the city, not moving the well.
Without loss, without gain,
They come and go, the well wells.
Almost drawn the water, but the rope does not quite reach the water,
Or breaking one's clay jug,
Pitfall.'

The people of ancient China would sometimes move a whole city to a more favourable site –
and they could take everything with them, except the well. You can transplant your centre and
change everything about your life, except for the source you draw on to sustain it all. You cannot
own this source, nor carry it with you; whenever you move, you will need first of all to dig a new
well to reach it.

    The well itself is utterly dependable: nothing anyone can do will raise or lower the water level.
People and experiences come and go; time passes; the well is always the well, and does not change.

    You need never doubt that you have these resources, or that they are enough. The real
question is whether you have the means to reach into such depths, and a steady hand to bring
the water up into the real world without loss. To fail would be disastrous. The potential in the
situation is undeniable, but it may still be a long way from realization.

Image

'Above the wood is the stream: the Well.
A noble one toils with the people, encouraging
them to help one another.'

If you could lean over an old Chinese well and look down
through the water, you would see a frame of logs at the bottom,
used to retain the silty soil as it was dug. The noble one is as

committed and involved in the well as the frame itself: inwardly as responsive as roots, outwardly pouring himself into the work like a flowing stream. The well is a vital shared resource; everyone must cooperate to build and maintain it.

Sequence

The Well follows from Hexagram 47, Confined:

'Confined in reaching upward naturally means turning inward, and so the Well follows.'

When you cannot reach upward and outward, you turn instead towards an inner source. The clear, life-giving water of the well is only to be found at the bottom of a very deep, dark pit.

CHANGING LINES

Line 1 *'The well is muddy, no drinking.*
Old well, no birds.'

There used to be a well here, but it has silted up. There is nothing here for you – no life – only some very sticky mud. Don't expect anything to come to, or from, this well.

Line 2 *'In the well's depths they shoot fish.*
The jug is cracked and leaking.'

At least the water is flowing clear, and there is some life and activity at the well. But people only experience the well's dark, isolating depths, and all they see in it is what they can believe in: a small, visible, immediate boon for themselves.

    Since it's hard to imagine a well in such poor repair becoming a permanent, dependable, shared source, people are not inclined to invest themselves in cooperative work to build such a thing. Hence there will be small fish, and no big crops. As they focus more narrowly on small personal gains, people may not even notice when a stray arrow cracks the well's jug.

Line 3 *'Well is dredged, no drinking.*
This makes my heart ache.
It can be used to draw water,
With the king's clear vision,
People together accept its blessing.'

The well has been dredged, and now the water can start to flow freely – *if only* people would see its potential and draw on it.

But it's important not to stay trapped in the pain of 'if only'. The well flows strongly, and all that's needed now is a guiding awareness strong and bright enough to illuminate its depths. If the leader recognizes the well and makes it plainly visible to all, the situation can be transformed into one of communication and blessing.

Line 4 *'Well is being lined,*
No mistake.'

A well dug in China's soft silt is a somewhat fragile thing: the walls could easily crumble into the water. To give it a dependable structure for the future, to ensure there will be a steady flow of clean water, the well needs to be lined.

This is a long-term undertaking – it will not be easy. The well may be out of commission altogether for a while; certainly there will be no immediate reward for your efforts. But even if it seems like too much to take on, lining your well, becoming more resourceful and making it easier to reach the well's full potential in future, is not a mistake.

Line 5 *'The well: clear, cold spring water to drink.'*

What you need is here: drink it. However dry and dusty your experience on the surface, you can be confident that reaching deep down into the well will connect you with a plentiful, natural source of cool water. You draw the water steadily, and then you can drink – how simple it is!

Line 6 *'The well gathers,*
Don't cover it.
There is truth and confidence,
Good fortune from the source.'

Water flows strongly into this well from underground sources. It's an image of effortless plenty: the water rising in the well, gathering more even as you draw from it – a constant, dependable flow.

It might seem safer to cover the well. You might want to hold yourself apart from the flow of receiving and giving, for fear of losing your freedom and autonomy in the constant exchange. Yet only when you remove the barriers and become part of the flow can you experience the true essence of the situation and tap into its deeper potential.

Hexagram 49, *Radical Change*

Key Questions

How can you break the mould?
How must the form change to express the essence?

Oracle

'Radical change.
On your own day, there is truth and confidence.
From the source, creating success, constancy bears fruit.
Regrets vanish.'

It is time for transformation. The old Chinese character for 'Radical Change', which also means 'leather', shows an animal hide: this is change like a shaman's, putting on a new skin to change your identity. And it is also revolutionary change: this hexagram marks the day when the Zhou people and their allies marched out to meet the armies of the corrupt Shang dynasty, and defeated them. You change the governing principle, and bring about renewal.

In the moment of change, there is truth — sincerity and a sure knowledge. Then the power of the whole unfolding creative process, from the source through to fruition and fulfilment, can enter here and change the world. Naturally regrets vanish, along with the past to which they belong. The new time is coming.

Image

'In the centre of the lake there is fire: Radical Change.
A noble one calculates the heavenly signs and clarifies the seasons.'

The new king must realign the calendar with the stars, bringing his people's daily activities back into harmony with the time. The light of awareness is at the centre of things, clear and unambiguous as starlight, and the calendar gives it expression. Inner lucidity illuminates and transforms a way of life — not bringing change for its own sake, but restoring a natural harmony.

Sequence

Radical Change follows from Hexagram 48, the Well:

'The way of the Well does not allow things not to change radically.'

Over time, human regimes fall out of harmony with the Way (*Dao*). Reconnecting with the unchanging source requires you to change the way you live.

Pair

Radical Change forms a pair with Hexagram 50, the Vessel:

'Radical Change puts away the old; the Vessel grasps renewal.'

Before you can found the new, you must remove the old. You may need to make deeper changes than you imagined.

CHANGING LINES

Line 1 *'Bound with yellow rawhide.'*
Radical Change has a long way to go – best to bind on your tough rawhide shoes very firmly before you set out. Your transformation begins as you put on this simple, practical, earth-coloured skin – not imagining things that are not yet real, but making yourself quite open to what is already real. This is the only place you can start, after all: with how things are, not how you would prefer them to be.

Though you are restlessly eager to be underway and initiating change, you find yourself bound by commitments, agreements and expectations. You have to honour the strength of these things, no matter how irksome they become. The oracle does not describe them as good or bad; they are simply there.

Line 2 *'Your own day, so make radical change*
And set out to bring order: good fortune, no mistake.'
This is your moment to begin the change, even if you cannot see exactly how things will turn out. By putting away the old, the things that do not belong, you can make a new way of living possible. Announce the new, and deal with the forces that threaten to sabotage it.

Line 3 *'Setting out to bring order means a pitfall,*
Constancy means danger.

> *As words of radical change draw near three times,*
> *There is truth and confidence.'*

What you are seeking is a change of mind. You cannot *make* this happen; awareness (other people's or your own) does not change just because you say it should. It's no use to try to impose order and take charge – to conquer – when you need a revolution to arise naturally and transform the whole organism. If you insist on carrying your own ideas through regardless, everything you have not enlisted will undermine you.

Instead, send words of change into circulation, and let them go round again and again. Change only happens once it has become part of awareness and an object of desire. It is this inner process, transforming speech and thought, that creates the unanimity and conviction that sustains a revolution.

Line 4 'Regrets vanish, there is truth and confidence.
Changing mandate, good fortune.'

You are ready; the revolution is already underway. You cannot regret the past when you inhabit the present moment, trusting the unfolding changes, and trusting yourself. This is the time when spiritual authority is taken from the old ruler and given to the new. So your guiding principles change, and with them your sense of what you are to do. The new will be better than the old.

Line 5 'Great person transforms as a tiger.
Even before the augury, there is truth and confidence.'

The great person, who has the power to carry things through, takes on the nature of a tiger.

Tigers have fluid strength, clear and vivid character, and sure-footed confidence. They do not tend to wait for confirmation or validation from outside. Unlike prey animals, they are not constantly reacting and fearful; they go where they choose.

As the tiger, you carry the power of your own truth within you, complete and clear in itself. You do not need a sign; you already know when and where to move.

Line 6 'Noble one transforms as a leopard,
Small people radically change their faces.
Setting out to bring order: pitfall.
Settling with constancy: good fortune.'

Your world, and your self, contain communities of noble and small people. Fundamental change comes naturally to the noble one, who takes the nature of the leopard and moves on with supple grace and strength. The small people would never initiate change themselves, but make superficial alterations to fit in with it as best they can.

So you will need the leopard's self-assurance to move independently of the small ones. You cannot force a comprehensive transformation and create the perfect world all at once – and to attempt this would be a disastrous distraction, critically weakening your core. This is a good time to settle down, focus on consolidating your central change, and foster harmony with your small people by allowing them space to adapt.

Hexagram 50, *the Vessel*

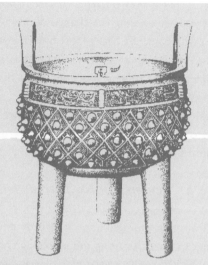

Key Questions

What is the vessel for transformation?
What are you beginning?
What will you cook?

Oracle

'The vessel.
Creating success from the source.
Good fortune.'

This marks a new beginning. The sacred Vessel is cast and used in the great ceremonies that inaugurate a new dynasty; the spirits are invited to share in the meal it contains, renewing their connection with the people. The Vessel provides stable, robust foundations for a new life, and also the crucible where you can expect to be transformed and remade.

The Vessel *contains and transforms*.

Just as wood becomes fire, or smelted ore becomes a great bronze vessel, or raw ingredients become fragrant food, so the experiences of life can be blended and transmuted into a meaningful whole.

Image

'Above wood there is fire: the Vessel.
A noble one sets the situation straight and consolidates her destiny.'

Fire rises from wood, and clarity arises from subtle inward receptivity. This is the cooking-place, the place for transmutation, and so the noble one works to bring it into harmony. She straightens out her situation – her relationships, especially, and where she stands overall.

This provides a good, stable basis for transformative work – a harmonious context where destiny can be realized. Inside a well-made Vessel, your sense of who you are and what you are here to do crystallizes and becomes clearly defined.

Sequence

The Vessel follows from Hexagram 49, Radical Change:

'For Radically Changing things, nothing equals the Vessel.'

It continues what Radical Change began, providing a secure space for transformation.

CHANGING LINES

Line 1   *'The vessel with upturned feet.*
     Fruitful to get the blockage out.
     Taking a concubine for her child,
     Not a mistake.'

Before you can access the whole rich potential for new beginnings, you have to clear out whatever old stuff is blocking communication and flow. The most important thing is to have the promise of new life and long-term growth – symbolized here by having a child.

So turn conventions and dignities upside down if you have to; do things that feel awkward and imperfect, if that's what it takes. Forfeiting some dignity won't really hurt you; the ends are far more important than the elegance of the means.

Line 2   *'The vessel contains something real.*
     My companions are afflicted,
     Cannot come near me.
     Good fortune.'

You have something real here. It is of genuine, solid value, and no diseased or negative mentalities can really touch it – whether they belong to other people, or to any inner 'companions' you may have (worries, desires, nagging little voices…).

These afflicted companions don't perceive the value of what you have: they just don't get it. That goes two ways: it means there is nothing here for them – they can't share in the vessel's riches and be nourished; also, it means that the contents of your vessel, your inner substance, cannot be infected or diminished – and this is good fortune.

Line 3   *'The vessel's ears are radically changed,*
     Its action blocked.
     Rich pheasant fat goes uneaten.
     Rain on all sides lessens regrets,
     In the end, good fortune.'

The vessel is being remade, and as its 'ears' – its carrying loops – are changed, it's not yet ready to be moved and used. This is like someone who is not open to connect with others. Even though there is good within them, it remains inaccessible, so people go unnourished and immediate needs are not met.

But this need not last. Rain will fall over all the fields of the realm, releasing tension and liberating blocked potential; seeds stirred from their dormancy will begin to grow. Regrets diminish little by little, in this larger view and longer term.

Line 4 *'The vessel's legs break off,*
The prince's stew is upset,
Dignity soiled.
Pitfall.'

Putting this vessel to use reveals its weakness: just when its stability is most needed, it collapses.

The vessel needs to be reinforced with commitment and devotion, upheld by strong, clear communication. These provide the strength to sustain a great responsibility. To have the vessel's supports fail at the key moment is deeply humiliating – and more than that, it is a disastrous omen for the future.

Line 5 *'The vessel with gold ears and bronze handle.*
Constancy bears fruit.'

The ears are loops on the rim of the vessel; the handle is a carrying-rod inserted through them. Together, they ensure the vessel can be moved and used.

Make your ears golden: purify and enrich your listening so that you become receptive to a more harmonious way of living. Precisely because it is available to be moved, the new order becomes stable and lasting. It can contain all the mysteries of what is to come, and will not be toppled by the unexpected.

Line 6 *'The vessel has a jade handle*
Great good fortune,
Nothing that does not bear fruit.'

Jade is the most precious material of all, and one that requires many hours and days of painstaking effort to shape and polish. Using it to craft the handle is a sign that the vessel is greatly honoured for its capacity to be moved – from place to place, and down through the ages.

A handle of jade will always be strong and softly lustrous; it will never tarnish. What you have here is immensely precious, not necessarily because of present circumstances, but because of the lasting value you can carry forward.

Hexagram 51, *Shock*

Key Questions

What must change?
What will continue?

Oracle

'Shock, creating success.
Shock comes, fear and terror.
Laughing words, shrieking and yelling.
Shock spreads fear for a hundred miles.
Someone does not lose the sacred ladle and libation.'

Shock is something that stirs, rouses and shakes you up – like an earthquake, or a violent thunderstorm. In ancient China, Heaven spoke through thunder, and this was an omen that the human world was to be brought back into harmony. Abruptly, your world is not working as you expect; the solid ground shifts under your feet, security slips away and mental constructs shatter; living reality has spoken.

Shock spreads out in waves of contagious fear and hysteria. Suddenly everyone is all too closely in touch with their own emotions – and with everyone else's – and all are reacting to one another.

It is a time to hold on to what you most value, and take on responsibility for keeping it safe through the upheaval, like the priest who is charged with safeguarding the temple and altars from the past, for the future. Consider what remains constant and true when everything else is in turmoil.

This doesn't necessarily mean resisting the shock itself, so much as keeping a still point in the midst of the tumult of reactions to it. Then you never lose your connection with the creative power that speaks through the storms.

Image

'Rolling thunder: Shock.
A noble one in fear and dread sets things in order and is watchful.'

When the outer world is shaken up, the noble one is also inwardly shaken. He is wide awake now, quivering with awareness of the changes underway, and ready to take on responsibility for restoring life to harmony.

Sequence

Shock follows from Hexagram 50, the Vessel:

'In the charge of the sacred vessel, none equals the eldest son, and so Shock follows. Shock means new beginnings.'

In the family of trigrams, thunder is the first son of heaven and earth, entrusted with the sacred vessel. As the old is overthrown and the new embraced, he stands at the gates and opens them to the new time. This brings both the emotional experience of shock, and also the awareness of a sacred connection that continues and is renewed through upheaval.

Pair

Shock forms a pair with Hexagram 52, Stilling:

'Shock begins; Stilling stops.'

Hexagram 51 sets things in motion and Hexagram 52 stills them. You are at a time of stirring and opening, yet the one who does not lose the ladle and libation is already keeping still.

CHANGING LINES

Line 1 *'Shock comes, fear and terror.*
Then afterwards, laughing words, shrieking and yelling. Good fortune.'
The worst part of this shock is your reaction to it. Then, as it passes by and you realize that you're still in one piece, your reaction shifts from terror towards excitement and relief.

    The line borrows words from the Oracle, but it specifies that the laughter comes *afterwards*. You begin to experience the shock as part of the passage of time, surveying it with hindsight and imagining it as part of your ongoing story. Then it leaves you more fully awake and alive, and with greater confidence.

Line 2 *'Shock comes, danger.*
A hundred thousand lost coins.
Climb up the nine hills, don't give chase.
On the seventh day, gain.'
Shock comes. There's nothing you can do about this, and to have things so utterly outside your control is disquieting in itself. Perhaps the most dangerous thing here is not what shocked you, but your reaction to

it. When you lose something you value greatly, it's important not to lose yourself and go rushing after it. You probably cannot see the whole picture, and you need a far better guide than the fear of loss.

So climb the nine hills: go to your source, where you have deep roots that outlast the shock and cannot be lost. Recover your self-possession and reconnect with your original intent. The world seen from here is so much bigger than what you have lost. In due course, the shock passes and the cycle turns, and though you lose what you had in mind, you gain something greater.

Line 3 *'Shock revives, revives.*
Shock moves without blunder.'

Shock comes upon you, bringing abrupt change. Let it bring you to life and stir you to action, awakening your inner vitality. If the change leaves you bemused and in the dark about which way to go, then let the shock itself be your guide and move along with it. The patterns of its action are meaningful in themselves; better to join with their energy than to resist them passively, as if reality were somehow a mistake. So respond to this shock as part of the fullness of life, and use it as a sign that this is time to act.

Line 4 *'Shock, and then a bog.'*

Rather than inspiring action, this shock gives rise to a whole quagmire of muddy emotions. You are bogged down and make no progress: you're stuck. Attempts to stir things up and create movement are likely just to create more mud. And yet, somewhere far behind or below the morass, where the shock shook you to the core, it might reawaken an inner awareness of the path, a faint sense of a quite different direction to go. But this is well buried, and not yet clear or strong enough to free you.

Line 5 *'Shock goes and comes, danger.*
Intention is not lost – there are things to do.'

Shock that comes on you in waves is especially disruptive; it makes it hard to gather yourself together and move forward. Yet these shocks also open up new possibilities to you, so that your heart's desire speaks more clearly than ever. The change re-energizes your intention, and also reveals that there is work to be done to realize it. You can harness the energy of the moment to get underway.

Line 6 *'Shock twists and turns,*
Watching in fear and terror,
Setting out to bring order: pitfall.
The shock does not reach your self, it reaches your neighbour –
No mistake. There are words of marital alliance.'

Shock tends to create shock, fear reacts to fear, and before long you are tying yourself in tortuous knots trying to keep track of it all. How can you cut through the turmoil and become effective again? Trying to conquer the unrest and impose order would be just one more reaction. Instead, among the chorus of panicking voices, find the self who remains untouched. Shock need not jolt you out of the flow of life altogether; you can reconnect, talking and thinking about ways to unite with the new and make it your ally.

Hexagram 52, *Stilling*

Key Questions

What if there were nothing you had to do now?
What if there were nowhere else you had to be?
Where is your inner point of balance?

Oracle

'Stilling your back,
Not grasping your self.
Moving in your rooms,
Not seeing your people.
Not a mistake.'

To still yourself is to come to rest in your own right place. It's not the opposite of motion, but of being pushed into motion by outside influences. Whether you move or stop is determined inwardly, by your sense of the nature of the time.

Attaining this kind of stillness means firmly, even stubbornly, resisting the forces that would disrupt your equilibrium. Hold yourself still, as if in meditation. Don't seek to 'grasp your self' by hunting down your every thought; you can no more make them stop by force of will than you can make your back still by holding it with your hands. Instead of twisting and spinning in circles trying to grasp your self, keep still.

In the same way, you can move freely in your rooms (or the chambers of your mind, which can be just as crowded) and simply not see the other people there, because you hold yourself still and do not resonate with them. Even if you feel as if you 'ought' to be constantly sensitive to their presence and needs, in a time of Stilling it is no mistake to exclude all these things, and be quiet within yourself.

Image

'Joined mountains: Stilling.
A noble one reflects, and does not come forth from his situation.'

Whatever upheavals take place around it, the mountain is still. The noble one in his environment is like two mountains – joined together, present to one another, and not reacting. He is still inwardly, and reflects; he is still outwardly, staying within his situation, not seeking to act on it or escape from it. Outer and inner stillness reinforce one another.

Sequence

Stilling follows from Hexagram 51, Shock:

'Things cannot end with stirring up; stop them. And so Stilling follows, which means stopping.'

There's a natural alternation between change and stillness. And in human experience, a time of Shock and reactions-to-reactions-to-reactions eventually needs to be stilled, change consolidated and equilibrium restored.

First the drum is struck, and the spreading vibrations set the whole drumhead quivering. Then you bring your hand down to damp the vibrations and still the drum.

CHANGING LINES

Line 1 *'Stilling your feet,*
         No mistake.
         Ever-flowing constancy bears fruit.'

It may feel as if people or events are forcing the issue so you have to take steps now. You don't. Slow down.

Become aware of your feet on the ground and create a moment of stillness. Standing firm, you rediscover your natural path and pace. You can flow on from here more consistently, in greater harmony with your environment and more genuinely connected with other people, because you are fully immersed in your authentic experience, not being bounced from one reaction to the next.

Line 2 *'Stilling your calves,*
         Not rescuing your following.
         Your heart not glad.'

Your calf muscles are just one connected part in a whole system of movement, so stilling them won't check your momentum altogether. It's as if you stop yourself moving forward, but you're standing on a moving surface: the whole situation is already underway, and this is stronger than your intention. You can't bring it to a complete stop, no matter how much you want to.

Your heart is not glad: your choice to be still does not give you true stillness; the direction of movement you're caught up in feels wrong, though it can't be helped. If only you had a firm place to stand.

Line 3 *'Stilling your waist,*
Dividing your back,
Danger smothers the heart.'

You want to move, but you stop yourself from acting on what you feel. Maybe you even try not to feel it at all, because you have the idea that you 'should' be still, or that you must hold yourself rigidly to a certain course.

By splitting your desires from your actions in this way, you tear yourself apart. The flow of communication from your heart to your body is cut off, and unfulfilled desires become like poisonous smoke, suffocating your capacity to feel or intend or choose.

Line 4 *'Stilling your self,*
No mistake.'

It may not be easy to find your place to stand. But to rediscover your poise and sense of power – without reacting, or fighting yourself for control – still your whole, undivided self. This brings you back in touch with who you are, where you are, and what you can do. Have confidence: from this still point, you will be effective. There is nowhere else you need to be.

Line 5 *'Stilling your jaws,*
Words have order,
Regrets vanish.'

When you still your jaws, you give yourself time to pause and reflect before using words – in speech or in thought. You don't blurt things out in reaction, or leap to conclusions, or make unfounded decisions.

Instead, your words, spoken or unspoken, have order: they are in harmony with your intent, and they move in clear sequence, observing what does and doesn't follow from their starting point. They set experience in a larger context, providing a sound foundation for the growth of understanding – something more than just reacting to circumstances. And so regrets for what has gone unresolved and unfulfilled gradually vanish away.

Line 6 *'Great-hearted stilling.*
Good fortune.'

To be still in your own integrity, compassionately embracing the autonomy of others without reacting to them, is the ultimate generosity. When you don't need anything from people or situations, you can see and accept them as they are – and offer them yourself as you are, instead of manufacturing responses you hope they might like. This is born of a very clear sense of your own distinct identity.

Hexagram 53, *Gradual Progress*

Key Questions

What is evolving here?
How can you be more patient?

Oracle

 'Gradual progress. The woman marries.
Good fortune.
Constancy bears fruit.'

'Gradual progress' is the name of an ancient river: it shows how water flows gradually and soaks through. The long ceremonial preparations for a woman's marriage progressed just as surely and gradually towards the moment when the bride could come home to her husband's house. And the moving lines of this hexagram tell the story of the wild geese, who mate for life, as they fly ever higher on their way home.

Bonds develop gradually, organically, as raw emotional energies are channelled into a lasting relationship. We grow into life's possibilities, and evolve and come home into our relationships. This yields results – gradually, almost imperceptibly – provided you have the patience to stay loyal to the destination as the journey unfolds.

Image

'On the mountain is a tree: Gradual Progress.
A noble one abides in virtuous character and improves the ordinary.'

The tree on the mountain grows very slowly compared to the one in the valley; it needs to put down strong roots. As it grows, it creates a micro-habitat around it, gradually, subtly changing the nature of its environment. The noble one's good character has the same effect, causing a gradual evolution in the habits of ordinary life. Inwardly as still and firm as the mountain, she settles into her high standards as if into a home, and reaches out in kindness like a growing tree.

Sequence

Gradual Progress follows from Hexagram 52, Stilling:

'Things cannot end with standstill, and so Gradual Progress follows. Gradual Progress means advancing.'

The unshakeable independence of Stilling is not an end in itself; it allows no space for growth, and growth cannot be stopped. Gradual Progress is founded in stillness, like the tree rooted in the mountain; the patience to sustain a growing relationship comes from self-sufficiency.

Pair

Gradual Progress is paired and contrasted with Hexagram 54, the Marrying Maiden:

'Gradual Progress: the marrying woman waits for the man to act.'
'Marrying Maiden: completion for the woman.'

These are two different experiences of marriage: the Marrying Maiden must adapt to a sudden change of state, but in a time of Gradual Progress you must *wait* – perhaps for a partner who moves at a slower pace, perhaps for some part of yourself to catch up with your resolution. For there to be a real union, the two must travel and arrive together.

CHANGING LINES

Line 1   *'Wild geese gradually progress to the shore.*
          The small child, danger. There are words – not a mistake.'

The wild geese have arrived at a border: a transition into new territory, where people must create new ways to live together. For this to become a true home, it needs a framework of clear relationships and boundaries. It is only within that framework that the child – whatever is small, vulnerable and growing – can be cared for and protected. So though the negotiations may be fraught or defensive, it is certainly not a mistake to work this out. The child has no safe place until agreement is reached.

Line 2   *'Wild geese gradually progress to the rock.*
          Drinking and eating, feasting and feasting. Good fortune.'

This is not a permanent place to stay, but it is secure enough for now, and it provides an opportunity to

rest and replenish your reserves for the journey ahead. This is a moment to enjoy: you can take pleasure in having enough, and being and sharing with other people. You can also use the time to re-orient yourself, getting a sense of where you are and what 'home' feels like, connecting with your inner guidance and discovering where you could go next. This is the beginning of a more lasting security.

Line 3 *'Wild geese gradually progress to the high plateau.*
The husband marches out and does not return,
The wife is pregnant, but does not raise the child.
Pitfall. Fruitful to resist outlaws.'

The high plateau is a strange new place, cold, bleak and exposed; we do not know how to live or find nourishment here. Partnership comes under terrible strain: someone may be too busy with other demands to protect the home; someone might be too preoccupied with inner processes to care for relationships: no-one meets their obligations.

You need to take a long view, right across the open plateau, so you can truly see other people, receive and protect them. You can best guard your home by warding off the forces of anger and violence, ensuring there is no way in for the self-centred, outlaw mindset.

Line 4 *'Wild geese gradually progress to the trees.*
Maybe find a flat branch – no mistake.'

This is not a comfortable perch; it will feel awkward, uncomfortable and hard to balance. But you do need to stop here for a while, concentrating on what's possible for now and not attempting to push on any further. Treat this as a temporary refuge, not a permanent place to stay.

Line 5 *'Wild geese gradually progress to the ancestral grave-mounds.*
The wife is not pregnant for three years.
In the end, nothing can prevent it. Good fortune.'

The ancestors are the foundation, the original deep-rooted energy of home. It's time to establish where you stand, reconnecting with a source that will sustain you – especially now your progress seems to be halted, with all the hope and preparation coming to nothing. But this need not be dramatized as a disaster: it's just a long delay before potential is realized.

Line 6 *'Wild geese gradually progress to the high plateau.*
Their feathers can be used to perform the sacred dances. Good fortune.'

It's hard to climb to such a high altitude, harder still to live in this cold, thin air. You cannot make an ordinary home here, or seek the kind of domestic, practical success you have imagined. Instead, you will need to conceive of a different kind of attainment and value.

The journey of the geese is drawing to its close: they vanish over the horizon, leaving a few feathers drifting down behind them. You are left with a gift to keep as part of your life – a symbol, a connection to something higher, the beginning of an imaginative transformation. Now that the story is over, and you are no longer living it chapter by chapter, it is time to learn to dance its whole meaning.

Hexagram 54, *the Marrying Maiden*

Key Questions

How can you grow into this situation?
What does it mean to you to come second?
How sustainable is this?

Oracle

*'The marrying maiden. To set out to bring order: pitfall.
No direction is fruitful.'*

A young girl, not yet a woman, comes home to her new husband's house. A nobleman of old China would marry his 'first wife' with great ceremony. She would go to her new home accompanied by a group of female relatives who became 'second wives'. These are the 'marrying maidens': they are present simply to make relationships easier and have no status of their own.

As a marrying maiden, you have accepted a relationship where you come second. You are only here to play a supporting role; it would be disastrous to try to shape the situation to fit your own needs. You are too junior, not yet ready to exert influence; there is no point in your setting intentions or making plans. All you can do is to feel your way, adapt, and find your place, without originating any action or having any agenda of your own.

Image

*'Above the lake, there is thunder: the Marrying Maiden.
A noble one through ever-flowing endings
Knows what wears out.'*

The lake is stirred and awoken by thunder, the vibrations travelling deep through the water. The noble one is inwardly as fluid as the lake, always open and responsive. So the shock of the new quickens her heart to a new awareness, and she senses the currents of change.

She sees how things that are complete are also flowing, like water, and this is how they endure – as the generations of a family endure. And as the spreading vibrations from the thunder reveal what is flawed, she also gains a direct and sure knowledge of what is too brittle to last.

Sequence

The Marrying Maiden follows from Hexagram 53, Gradual Progress:

'Making progress must mean a time to come home, and so the Marrying Maiden follows.'

To 'come home' also means 'to marry', and Gradual Progress is associated with the ceremonies of marriage. However gradual or careful the preparations, now comes the moment of transition into a new life.

Instead of being able to change her circumstances gradually to keep pace with her inner development, the Marrying Maiden has to develop herself to catch up with the sudden and complete change in her circumstances.

CHANGING LINES

Line 1 *'Maiden marries as a younger sister.*
Lame, can still walk.
Setting out to bring order: good fortune.'

You start out at a disadvantage, labouring under a handicap. But the important thing is that you do start out. There may be some things you cannot fix or heal, and some things that will never come easily – but when you are aware of your limitations, and understand how hard this will be, then it is good to take charge and set to work.

As you do what you can, those disadvantages and handicaps lose their power to trap you in 'I can't'. You find the freedom to move and create change.

Line 2 *'With one eye, can see.*
A hermit's constancy bears fruit.'

With one eye, you have a single and undivided point of view; you focus to the exclusion of all distractions. The disadvantage, of course, is that your perception is limited: you do not see the whole picture, or not in three dimensions.

If you locate your security outside yourself when your vision is so limited, you can expect some unpleasant surprises. It is better to be like the hermit: self-sufficient, not attempting to change the situation, but staying quietly loyal to your own insight. The hermit has inner independence; she is the same person whether or not anyone is watching.

Line 3 *'Marrying maiden waiting,*
Turns it round and marries as second wife.'

The maiden entering into marriage is full of energy, and wants very much to express it and find fulfilment. For the sake of being included and having a place, she will accept even a very lowly position. Provided she is patient and does not try for too much, she can turn things to her advantage and even change her situation: she cannot gain the first position, or take control, but she may be able to exert an indirect influence.

Line 4 *'Marrying maiden overruns the set time.*
Delays and marries at the right time.'

There is time measured from the outside, in deadlines, schedules, a well-constructed framework of expectations that lays out when change and progress should happen. And there is time as it is known from the inside, when the right moment arises by itself.

To 'marry' and come home to your own place needs to happen at the right time. It is important to support the natural process of growth towards completion, rather than committing yourself for fear of missing something.

Line 5 *'King Yi marries off the maidens.*
The first wife's sleeves are not as fine as the younger sister's.
The moon almost full, good fortune.'

King Yi was a late Shang ruler, who gave his daughters in marriage to the Zhou. The younger sister's fine sleeves are a promising sign of her fertility; she was to be the one who bore an important son, probably King Wen himself.

You have reached a place where you can grow into your potential and eventually be of greater service; your spirit shines through, stronger than precedent. The moon almost full is a sign of the greater strength of what is still growing, compared to what is already at its peak. You can look forward to ongoing light and growth.

Line 6 *'The woman offers a basket with no contents.*
The gentleman sacrifices a goat with no blood.
No direction bears fruit.'

The partners should bring full, living offerings for their marriage; here there is nothing but dead, empty forms. Neither partner is committed; both withhold what they have. With such a lack of belief and trust, there is no relationship – nothing to sustain the connection, and nowhere for it to go.

Hexagram 55, *Abundance*

Key Questions

What are you called on to do?
What decisions must you take now?

Oracle

'Abundance, creating success.
The king assumes it.
Do not mourn. A fitting sacrifice at noon.'

This is a cornucopia, a wealth of resources – but also a wealth of choices, tasks and demands.
This is the crucial moment, where it all comes together.
The name of the hexagram, Abundance (*Feng*), is also the name of the garrison city where King
Wen made final preparations for the overthrow of the Shang rulers. There, Wen died, and his son
Wu had to decide whether to observe the prescribed period of mourning in isolation, or take
command of the armies at once.

He was given a sign: a total eclipse of the sun at noon. Divination revealed that it was not time
for Wu to mourn: he had received Heaven's Mandate to conquer the Shang, and should make the
right offering to the earth in preparation for war, so the darkness of Shang rule would come to
an end.

In a time of Abundance you find that, despite what you have lost, there is a new charge given to
you that leaves no place for sorrow or anxiety. It is not the time to hide yourself away and grieve
the past. Decide what you will do, take it on, make the practical preparations and march out.

Image

'Thunder and lightning culminate as one:
Abundance.
A noble one decides legal proceedings and
brings about punishment.'

Thunder and lightning come together: the storm is
directly overhead. It is time for inner clarity to become
action – to take the decision, and accept the consequences.

Sequence

Abundance follows from Hexagram 54, the Marrying Maiden:

'Attaining the place where you belong naturally means greatness, and so Abundance follows.'

The marrying maiden finds her new home in her husband's house. You may not have asked for your new situation, you may not be ready for it, but it is yours to grow into and make your own.

Pair

Abundance forms a pair with Hexagram 56, Travelling:

'Abundance has many causes; few connections for the Traveller.'

These show two ways of being at the centre, responsible for making the decisions. The Traveller is on his own; but here, you are at the centre of an abundance of resources, plans and allies, feeling the weight of everything that led up to this point.

CHANGING LINES

Line 1   *'Meeting your partner and lord,*
Though for ten days, no mistake.
Going on brings honour.'

You encounter your match and counterpart, someone you can join with in alliance. Such an alliance is not meant to be a lifelong partnership; it is important not to presume on its strength and overstep its bounds.

    This doesn't make the meeting insignificant, or a waste; it is important – and also has a natural time limit. ('Ten days' stands for any finite span of time.) Afterwards, you take whatever you received and learned from the encounter, and move on.

Line 2   *'Feng is screened off.*
At midday, seeing the Dipper.
Going on gains doubts and anxieties.
With truth and confidence coming to expression,
Good fortune.'

The eclipse begins, and you are cut off from the light. It is dark when the day should be brightest; you can't see where you are. Of course you are fearful and uncertain, and it is very hard to act decisively.

But you can orientate yourself by the bright stars of the Dipper. Although you don't see and understand what's happening in the normal way, you *can* see which way to go. You need only trust your insight and act on it, like Wu, empowered to decide by the Mandate.

Line 3 *'Feng is flooded with darkness,*
At midday, seeing a froth of light.
Your right arm broken - not a mistake.'

The eclipse reaches totality; there is utter darkness at noon, with only faint light (perhaps from the solar corona).

You are left in complete confusion and bewilderment, with nothing to navigate by. Your ability to act, or your most important support, is taken away. Yet this is not a bad thing: perhaps it keeps you out of trouble. You don't need to prove yourself by taking action straight away.

Line 4 *'Feng is screened off*
At midday, seeing the Dipper.
Meeting your hidden lord - good fortune.'

The sun is eclipsed; you are cut off from the light. You can still orient yourself by the bright stars of the Dipper – you're aware of the direction you want to travel in – but you cannot see to move forward.

The hidden lord you meet here is dark, maybe threatening, and not someone (or something) you would normally perceive as a potential ally. But because of the importance of what you have to do, you will meet what you fear – and because you can see your direction so clearly, you can bring even the hidden lord into alliance with your greater purpose.

Line 5 *'A thing of beauty coming*
Brings reward and praise, good fortune.'

A beautiful new creation is being chosen and designed here. This is to be celebrated! Just as Wu's experience at Feng heralded the coming of the Zhou dynasty, this can usher in a whole new order, and bring the gift of confidence and independent strength.

Line 6 *'At Feng, in his hut,*
Screening off his home, peeping through his door.
In solitude, without people, for three years sees no-one.
Pitfall.'

The signs of what to do are emerging, and the demands on you are clear – all too clear, and all too many. You're inclined to shut yourself away and block it all out. You become oblivious to others, absorbed in your own, private, altogether more manageable world.

Imagine if Wu had shut himself away in his hut to observe the full ritual mourning, instead of accepting the Mandate and marching out. Would the great change ever have happened?

Hexagram 56, *Travelling*

Key Questions

What do you bring with you into each new situation?
What does this place ask of you?

Oracle

'Traveller, creating small success.
Travelling, constancy brings good fortune.'

The traveller is on a journey of his own, just passing through this place and staying for a while. To be the traveller means you are not at home here – you know you don't belong. Also, you have a strong personal direction: wherever you find yourself for now, you know it does not define you.

As the traveller, you might be like King Hai, an early leader of the Shang. His people were nomads, who stopped to pasture their animals at a place called Yi ('Change'). They were welcomed by the local people – until Hai danced for their ruler and seduced his wife. Then the Yi ruler had Hai executed and took his herds, and his people fled.

Since you are only passing through, your creative involvement is limited. You can have the small success of being well received if you fit in responsively, rather than dancing your own dance regardless of where you are. You cannot expect to change your surroundings – and nor should your surroundings change you: it is good to be constant to your own way as you travel. As Hai discovered, this can be a difficult balance to keep: to be true to yourself, and still fit in to a place that is not your own.

Image

'Above the mountain is fire: Travelling.
A noble one is clear and thoughtful in administering punishments, and doesn't draw out legal proceedings.'

The fire above the mountain is like a camp fire. Before its limited fuel is exhausted and the flames die down, any disputes must be resolved; then

the travellers will be free to move on next day. So a noble one completes things with the firmness of a mountain, and uses the clarity of fire to cast light on decisions and endings. You have neither the resources nor the time to get embroiled in long drawn-out wranglings, either with yourself or with others.

Sequence

Travelling follows from Hexagram 55, Abundance:

'Exhausting greatness naturally means letting your dwelling place go, and so Travelling follows.'

In the time of Abundance, you were at the centre of your domain, with a great wealth of resources, demands and responsibilities coming to you. Now that time is over; you leave home behind and carry your small uniqueness out into the larger world.

CHANGING LINES

Line 1 *'The traveller – fragmented and bitty,*
Chops up his place and courts disaster.'
The traveller is narrowly focused on the details of immediate experience, and fails to see them in their larger context. Perhaps he divides his attention among too many areas at once – or he may be concentrating exclusively on analysing the details of just one little thing. He breaks up the situation into lots of little bits, so that the big picture and the purpose of the journey are lost to view altogether.

   This could be the beginnings of self-sabotage, setting yourself up for future disaster. What effect does it have on your overall wellbeing and security when a focus on the pieces distracts you from the whole?

Line 2 *'Traveller comes to a resting place,*
Cherishes his own,
Gains a young helper.
Constancy.'
You've come to a safe resting place, but not arrived home. Like the traveller who keeps his valuables safely on his person, your most precious assets are still those you carry with you, which do not depend on the circumstances or responses you meet in these foreign places. You stay loyal to your own ongoing journey, find good help and support, and continue steadily on your way.

Line 3 *'Traveller burns down his resting place.*
Loses his young helper.
Constancy: danger.'

On your journey, you find shelter for a while, and help. But out of a burning desire for more – more security, more fulfilment, more energy – than is possible in such a place, you destroy it. Likewise, your intensity and eagerness to make progress means you lose helpful relationships. It's as if, oblivious to the small lodge where you find yourself, you tried to light a huge hearth fire.

This is certainly constancy to the journey: if you burn all your bridges, you leave yourself no choice but to keep moving. But it's a dangerous habit for a traveller, in the long run, to keep setting fire to his refuges in a blaze of ambition.

Line 4 *'Traveller in a place to stay,*
Gains property and an axe.
My heart is not glad.'

You have your place, and to some extent you have what you sought, but you are not at home here; you haven't found help or rest. The position feels unnatural and insecure, and you have to be constantly on the defensive to maintain it. You cannot enjoy what you have.

Line 5 *'Shooting a pheasant,*
Gets it with one arrow.
So in the end, praise and a mandate.'

If the traveller can demonstrate his skill and take a gift to the local lord, he will gain recognition and employment.

Having a 'mandate' could be as sublime as a spiritual calling, or as mundane as a job, but it does mean you have useful work to do. This is a time to be as direct as an arrow's flight: see what is needed that you can do, and be single-minded in doing it. This is how you will find security: you are at home where you can be of service.

Line 6 *'The bird burns its nest.*
Travelling people first laugh, afterwards cry out and weep.
Lose cattle in Yi.
Pitfall.'

King Hai put on feathers and danced – and burned his nest.

You are accepted, even welcomed, but your relationships here are far more fragile than you realize. You can easily become over-confident, go too far, and destroy them – and then you lose everything.

Hai danced his own dance at Yi. This is authentic self-expression, heedless of your environment, not connecting with other people or considering their expectations. When you do things your own way and on your own terms, and assume (or demand) that others will adapt, this is satisfying at first, and utterly disastrous in the end.

Hexagram 57, *Subtly Penetrating*

Key Questions

How can you get to know this from the inside?
What is taking shape?

Oracle

'Subtly penetrating, creating small success.
Fruitful to have a direction to go,
Fruitful to see the great person.'

Subtly penetrating means becoming part of something, or someone. It describes all-pervading influences, like the wind shaping the landscape.

You penetrate subtly by feeling your way into things, yielding gently to their nature. You shift your own ideas and expectations, and come to understand the situation from inside, on its own terms. And so, as you allow things to shape you, you also reach a place where you can shape them.

The old Chinese character for 'Subtly Penetrating' shows a stand bearing the official seals a ruler would bestow on those he trusted. Someone who bows down and accepts a seal is submitting to the order of things, entering in and receiving his place within it. Then his seal, sign of personal authenticity, endows him with influence and the power to 'make his mark'.

Whatever penetrates subtly becomes influential – not by acting *on* situations or people to change their nature, but by becoming part of their nature and acting *in* them. Because it never acts as an antagonist, it never creates resistance and permeates everywhere.

Such influence does not bring sudden transformations: it works imperceptibly, in tiny increments, only creating small success. It is useful to align all these small shifts with a single intention that lends direction to the changes. And, whether you see them in the flesh or with your inner eye, it's good to have a clear vision of the great person – a model of the larger possibilities implied by small success.

Image

'Wind follows wind: Subtly Penetrating.
A noble one conveys mandates and carries
out the work.'

Winds beget winds, movement creates movement and the influence penetrates everywhere. This is a time to use your own inner 'seal of office' – to translate what moves you inwardly into your influence in the world. When a noble one receives a mandate, she conveys it onward by sending out orders, and so her indirect influence reaches further than direct action ever could.

Sequence

Subtly Penetrating follows from Hexagram 56, Travelling:

'The Traveller has no place where he is accepted, and so Subtly Penetrating follows. Subtly Penetrating means entering in.'

The traveller followed his own path and minimized his interaction with his surroundings, not expecting to change them or be changed by them. But presently, the traveller must come home: there is a time for acceptance, and the interpenetration of inner and outer worlds.

Pair

Subtly Penetrating forms a pair with Hexagram 58, Opening:

'Opening: seeing. Subtly Penetrating: hidden away.'

Some things are in plain view; some are hidden away. Among people there is explicit communication, and there is the subtle interpenetration of lives in countless small ways.

CHANGING LINES

Line 1 *'Advancing, withdrawing.*
   A warrior's constancy is fruitful.'
You try to enter and find your place, but you experience setbacks as well as progress. Sometimes the most adaptive, intelligent response is to withdraw. You can stay true to your chosen direction like a warrior, who sees all advances and retreats in the context of a single purpose, and is not discouraged.

Line 2 *'Subtly penetrating under the bed,*
   Using historians and diviners of many kinds.

Good fortune, no mistake.'

You need to get to know what you rest on and what it's made of. You'll need to use a whole variety of modes of perception and ways of understanding to discover all the different influences at work. At first, this brings a confusion of information and insights – hard to assimilate, especially if you feel an urgent need to change things. But understanding will develop gradually from these beginnings: as you become aware of how it all fits together, you create a secure, stable foundation for future growth.

Line 3 *'Subtly penetrating with urgency – shame.'*

You are pushing for a response. Instead of adapting when you don't find what you need, you try again, neurotically probing for something more substantial. You seek certainty where there is none to be had: insisting on this, as if you had something to prove, is ultimately exhausting and leads to humiliation.

Line 4 *'Regrets vanish. In the field, taking three kinds of game.'*

Not all you hope for comes to you – but as you allow your regrets to dissolve away, you can enter into the present moment, with all its uncertainties, in the positive spirit of the hunt. You broaden your scope to see the many different possibilities available to you, and gain all you need.

Line 5 *'Constancy, good fortune, regrets vanish.*
Nothing that does not bear fruit.
With no beginning, there is completion.
Before threshing, three days.
After threshing, three days.
Good fortune.'

When you are always seeking to understand and enter in, not only do you gain valuable understanding, but there comes a moment when this understanding enables you to bring about positive change. The origins of the situation are hidden away, and it may seem unpromising at first. Yet there can be real achievement when you penetrate to the core of the matter, and also *bring out* what is valuable, discarding the useless chaff. Where previously you were feeling your way, now you make things clear.

This isn't accomplished all at once, but by carefully, attentively bringing things into awareness and setting them in a broader context. You need to allow time to consider what led up to this moment and what is taking shape now – and also, after the kernel is uncovered, to consider how it changes things, and how you will respond to it. There is a real opportunity here to change everything for the better.

Line 6 *'Subtly penetrating under the bed,*
Losing your property and axe.
Constancy, pitfall.'

There is no limit to the possibilities you could explore – but in your endless search for certainty, you lose what you value, and forfeit your power to make any one possibility real. You scrutinize circumstances (especially what others think and want) as if these were determining factors in the outcome. This will not help you make a decision; instead, it becomes a way of surrendering your authority to act.

Hexagram 58, *Opening*

Key Questions

How can you fully enjoy the moment?
What are you bringing to expression?
What if you communicated and exchanged more freely?

Oracle

'Opening, creating success.
Constancy bears fruit.'

The early Chinese character for 'Opening' shows someone with words rising from their mouth: they seem to be dancing and singing. It means joyful and outgoing expression that opens up communication.

Opening brings people together and begins a lively creative process of sharing and exchange. It liberates human energies, motivates people to overcome hardship and encourages perseverance.

Image

'Lakes joined together: Opening.
A noble one joins with friends to speak and practise together.'

Two joined lakes, open to one another, flow together freely and enrich one another. The same is true of friends who join together to discuss and share their understanding: the exchange of ideas and pooling of insights makes everyone richer.

Sequence

Opening follows from Hexagram 57, Subtly Penetrating:

'Entering in and then rejoicing, and so Opening follows.'

You subtly penetrate things and know them from the inside; then you bring things out and express them with joy, taking delight in the freedom to interact and connect.

CHANGING LINES

Line 1 *'Responsive opening, good fortune.'*
This is the promising beginning of conversation: not mere self-expression, but the capacity to listen and respond. You foster trust, and make mutual enrichment possible, by opening up your inner space to exchange.

The foundation for this responsive communication is autonomy and self-reliance: it means that you have something to give, and that you can create a harmonious connection that is not dominated or distorted by what people *need* from one another.

Line 2 *'True and confident opening, good fortune.*
Regrets vanish.'
This means opening up a clear channel for honest communication where people are wholly present. When you can speak with true conviction of what is valuable here, regrets dissolve away. You move fully into the present moment, sensing and communicating how its currents are flowing.

Line 3 *'Coming opening, pitfall.'*
'Coming opening' means looking expectantly for what you want to come to you, easily and on your own terms. You try to dictate how things will be; this doesn't work. The joy you seek can't simply come to you from outside, but only arises from authentic exchange.

Line 4 *'Negotiating opening, not yet at rest.*
Containing the affliction brings rejoicing.'
You're considering and discussing a change, and you want to settle all the details before you commit yourself, so you can be sure of how things will work and more confident that you're making the right decision.

You're also under great pressure to decide. This magnifies your restlessness into deep anxiety; unless you set some limits to this, it will tend to take over and turn the negotiations into obsessive haggling.

If you rest secure in the knowledge of what you want and need, you can reach your decision calmly, in your own time. You'll also find that participating in the interplay of negotiation enriches you, and the dance of exchange is something you can enjoy.

Line 5 *'Trusting in stripping away,*
There is danger.'

You place your trust in something unreliable, with risks you're quite unaware of. You might be forfeiting your authority and autonomy here. *Perhaps*, to move to a new level of experience, you might need to open yourself more . . . but this is a dangerous idea if it leads you to surrender control. Where are you placing your trust, and why?

Line 6 *'Opening that pulls.'*

This is communication that draws you in, part of an ongoing relationship and exchange with powerful attractive forces. It can feel as if you are being guided – but Yi doesn't say whether or not your direction is a good one. You are not seeing too clearly yourself; the attraction is strong, but what you are drawn to may or may not be attainable here.

Hexagram 59, *Dispersing*

Key Questions

Where and how can you be less rigid?
Where were the walls in this situation, and what can you see as they dissolve away?
As energy and vitality is liberated from old boundaries, where will it go?

Oracle

'Dispersing, creating success.
The king assumes his temple.
Fruitful to cross the great river,
Constancy bears fruit.'

It is as if a great thaw brought the floods, and everything solid were swept away. All the walls – whether they divided, contained or sheltered – are gone. The familiar landmarks have vanished down the river, and there's a clear view for miles over free-flowing waters. Perhaps this liberates the vital energy of the situation; perhaps it is utterly disorientating.

Definitions, dividing lines, agreements, bonds, established patterns of life and thought . . . all these can be Dispersed, their solidity revealed as an illusion. All that holds things together now is the constancy of the flow itself.

The king 'assumes' his temple: he draws near and enters it, and takes on his most important role as the people's connection to spirits and ancestors. This can also be an inner process: centring your inner authority in your spiritual home; letting your decisions flow from that essential underlying source.

With this reconnection, it becomes possible to 'cross the great river' – which has already come to you. The dissolution of the old forms releases energy into new purpose and direction; staying true to the deep connection through the temple, it's good to make the commitment and venture into the unknown.

Image

'Wind moves above the stream: Dispersing.
The ancient kings made offerings to the Highest to establish
the temples.'

Wind moving above the stream stirs and disperses it as water vapour – reminiscent of the fragrant steam that rises from the offerings and nourishes the spirits. This is the real substance of things: the inner flow of committed offering, the message and influence spreading outward. What is established with offerings will endure, while what is built of rock crumbles away. What are you building on?

Sequence

Dispersing follows from Hexagram 58, Opening:

'Rejoicing and hence scattering it, and so Dispersing follows. Dispersing means spreading out.'

Active, joyful communication and exchange naturally loosens things up and tends towards complete Dispersing: full visibility, with no boundaries, distinctions or focus.

Pair

Dispersing forms a pair with Hexagram 60, Measuring:

'Dispersing means spreading out; Measuring means stopping.'

Dispersing has no limits that would stop its flow – yet eventually this liberated energy will flow on into new, more organic forms.

CHANGING LINES

Line 1 *'Rescuing with a horse's strength.*
Good fortune.'
As you first become aware that things are dispersing – or that some things *need* to be dispersed – it's already time to act. Using the resources and power available to help the situation now will make a key difference: there is enough strength to get free, enough buoyancy to stay afloat. That might mean 'staging a rescue'; it might also mean that an inner experience of dispersing lends you strength.

Line 2 *'Dispersing, flee to your support.*
Regrets vanish.'

Amidst the swirling uncertainties of Dispersing, what are you still sure of? Perhaps an essential truth comes into view now; perhaps you can simply see more clearly what will work. Grasp this, and there will no longer be any need to regret what was lost: it turns out that what you have is all you need for now.

Line 3 *'Dispersing your self*
Without regrets.'

At the surface, the water evaporates into the wind. Your little self can disperse now, as you quietly enter into a larger self and deeper truth, one where your independence and what you 'stand for' are no longer so important. As your identity disperses and expands, there is nothing to be anxious about; nothing real is lost.

Line 4 *'Dispersing your flock,*
From the source, good fortune.
Dispersing gains the hilltop,
No barbarian has occasion to think of this.'

The flock will always, automatically, move together along established paths. To disperse the flock, to challenge 'flock mentality' with more expansive thinking, means good fortune from the source. Original thought will find a 'hilltop' that offers longer perspectives and stronger roots. The ordinary mindset, though, that can only react to challenge by reaching for its weaponry, lacks the mental space to conceive of these new dimensions.

Line 5 *'Dispersing sweat, his great proclamation.*
Dispersing the king's residence,
Not a mistake.'

This is a time of such intensity that the ruler's words must be charged with power, as if his own essence were dispersed and flowed out through them like sweat. This is unknown territory; the only way to learn is to act.

And so even the king's residence, the fixed point at the centre of it all, will be dispersed. Close by are the granaries, which the king could open to the people in times of great crisis or transition. To respond adequately now requires that you disperse whatever central reserves you might still be holding on to; you can put it all into circulation.

That may feel like giving up everything that offered you some chance of control, security or stability, and yet it is 'not a mistake'; it demonstrates commitment and real strength.

Line 6 *'Dispersing blood.*
Leave, go out and far away.
Not a mistake.'

It's possible to dissolve one boundary too many; some things, like blood, are better kept on the inside. When all barriers are down and anything is thinkable, when blood – or vital energy, or extreme emotion – starts to flow, you are very vulnerable. Don't over-commit yourself and become trapped here; get to a safe distance.

Hexagram 60, *Measuring*

Key Questions

What limits apply here?
What agreements are at work?
Does everyone understand them and find them palatable? Do you?

Oracle

'Measuring, creating success.
Bitter measures do not allow for constancy.'

Things need to be articulated to make them more
manageable, easier to take in and work with. Such
measures, when they grow organically, reflect the natural
rhythms of life and allow a fuller participation in its flow.
Progress is made in small increments.

Individuals with measure live sustainably and flourish; groups
who share measures and standards, who speak the same language, can
reach agreement and build trust. But if anyone reacts to the measures as
they would to a bitter taste – if they find them too hard to swallow – then
they are not sustainable. This isn't a matter of tradition, principle or logic,
but of human experience.

Image

'Above the lake is the stream: Measuring.
A noble one works out and reckons the measures,
Reflecting on character in action.'

The streams flow into the lake and out from it – but how much
water can the lake hold? Or how many channels can we dig leading
out from it before there is insufficient water to reach our fields?

A noble one will work out these limits to capacity and flow by discovering what works in practice. He is like the lake that reflects and deepens, and like the streams that flow out and reveal a character's depth and resource through action.

Sequence

Measuring follows from Hexagram 59, Dispersing.

'Things cannot end with spreading out, and so Measuring follows.'

When artificial limits have dissolved away, it's time to develop organic, authentic ones. People need boundaries.

CHANGING LINES

Line 1 *'Not going out of the door to the family rooms.*
Not a mistake.'

You can stay within your own capacity and your own space. Even if you feel trapped, there's actually no need to go out to find solutions. It's better to stay inside your boundaries.

Line 2 *'Not going out of the gate from the courtyard.*
Pitfall.'

This gate leads from the family rooms to the street outside. Inside is the known and familiar, a restricted range of stimulus and nourishment, and an equally restricted range of options. This home base is a good centre from which to explore, but for it to become the outer limit of your world is unhealthy and constricted. Out beyond your usual boundaries, where you don't know what to expect, there is room for growth.

Line 3 *'No measure, and hence lamenting.*
Not a mistake.'

If you don't set some limits to your hopes, desires and expectations, if you don't enter into down-to-earth conversation (with yourself, with other people, with circumstances) about what's possible, then you will lament.

Yet Yi says this is 'not a mistake' – perhaps because such intense emotion cannot be judged, perhaps just because this is a chance to learn.

Line 4 *'Peaceful measures.*
Creating success.'

You have your house in order; you know what's needed and what to ask for. There is no need to be anxious or try too hard; you are on your own ground, where you can interact calmly.

Line 5 *'Sweet measures, good fortune.*
Going on brings honour.'

This is the opposite of those 'bitter measures' the Oracle speaks of. It tastes good: these are rules that allow you to enjoy life, like the good manners of friendly conversation. Sweet measures bring good fortune just because they *do* allow constancy, and are a good starting point for future growth.

Line 6 *'Bitter measures: constancy, pitfall.*
Regrets vanish.'

The truth of the situation will not fit into the rules, definitions or stories you're trying to impose on it. Constancy is not possible with such bitter measures; to try to make it all work regardless means misfortune.

Sooner or later, the bitter measures will prove untenable and the truth will reassert itself. Then regrets vanish – because what is not in accord with truth was never real at all.

Hexagram 61, *Inner Truth*

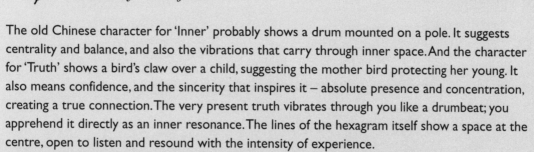

Key Questions

Where do you place your trust?
What feels true?

Oracle

'Inner truth. Piglets and fishes, good fortune.
Fruitful to cross the great river.
Constancy bears fruit.'

The old Chinese character for 'Inner' probably shows a drum mounted on a pole. It suggests centrality and balance, and also the vibrations that carry through inner space. And the character for 'Truth' shows a bird's claw over a child, suggesting the mother bird protecting her young. It also means confidence, and the sincerity that inspires it – absolute presence and concentration, creating a true connection. The very present truth vibrates through you like a drumbeat; you apprehend it directly as an inner resonance. The lines of the hexagram itself show a space at the centre, open to listen and resound with the intensity of experience.

Piglets and fishes are symbols of wealth, plenty and luck. They are staple foods used in humble offerings to the spirits: to receive piglets and fishes shows that you are in a state of connectedness, and can trust you will be provided for. Success in ongoing ventures (rearing your pigs), and the insight to be in the right place at the right time (placing the fishing nets) are both manifestations of your inner truth. And so it is good to commit yourself: inner truth will naturally move you towards new landscapes, as the inner hollow of a boat would carry you across the water. You stay true to your understanding by carrying it through into action, translating the moment of insight into responsiveness as a constant way of living.

Image

'Above the lake is the wind: Inner Truth.
A noble one deliberates over legal proceedings and delays executions.'

The wind reaches and influences everywhere, always bringing new messages of change. The open surface of the lake, stirred by the wind, is constantly in motion. As the lake doesn't set hard into a final shape, so the noble one is slow to take irreversible decisions. To be true, she stays fluid and open, allowing herself to be moved by changing circumstances and new perspectives.

Sequence

Inner Truth follows from Hexagram 60, Measuring:

'Measuring and also trusting it, and so Inner Truth follows.'

By clearly defining agreements, Measuring makes trust possible. When people share a way of measuring and understanding, a mental map, they can trust one another; when the map corresponds with reality, they enjoy a trustworthy connection with the world.

Pair

Inner Truth is paired and contrasted with Hexagram 62, Small Exceeding:

'Small Exceeding steps over the line; Inner Truth means trust.'

With Inner Truth, you have complete confidence; things feel stable and dependable. Small Exceeding is the opposite experience: stepping out into the world, feeling small, exposed and out of balance, constantly aware of the need to adapt.

CHANGING LINES

Line 1 *'Guided, good fortune.*
There is another, no peace.'
Inner truth is opening up a flow of change; existing frameworks and agreements of all kinds can no longer be taken for granted. There is guidance available that can lead you towards good fortune – but it's as well to be vigilant for other factors that may complicate matters and disturb your peace: half-hidden needs or beliefs, other people's influence, or divergent, mutually incompatible desires.

Line 2 *'Calling crane in the shadows,*
Her young respond in harmony.
I have a good wine vessel,

I will share with you, pouring it all out.'
The crane calls from a hidden place, inviting connection, and her young respond; a graceful, bird-shaped wine vessel is poured out in friendship. There is complete and unreserved sharing, like the love of parent and child; any information conveyed here is far less important than the simple presence of communication that can reach across any distance. Whether or not this moment endures, it is a true connection of souls, and a blessing in itself.

Line 3 *'Gaining a counterpart.*
Maybe drumming, maybe resting.
Maybe weeping, maybe singing.'

You join with your counterpart – a person or situation that acts as your match and mirror – in a pattern of mutual reaction. Everything is reflected back and magnified; advance is followed by retreat, and exaggerated emotions veer between extremes. This is not communication: dialogue, inner or outer, would need more space. Instead, there is a great intensity of experience, its volatile emotions not quite mastered. Yi does not say if this is good or bad.

Line 4 *'The moon almost full,*
A horse's yoke-mate runs away.
No mistake.'

The light is growing: what is new and still in potential is stronger than what is old and well established. This is the cusp of change, and there is good light to travel by.

A horse that has been part of a team runs away: drawn towards greater authenticity, you separate from a companion and become free to find your own way. You leave behind whatever kept you moving in a predetermined direction, realizing that you are not required to carry on: there is no necessary connection. Even if you feel some nostalgia for what you leave behind, nothing is wrong.

Line 5 *'There is truth and confidence as a bond – no mistake.'*
The very fact that you are true binds you in presence, sincerity and trust. You have to give things up in and for this bond: in particular, you let go everything you desired or imagined that is not available within it. Yet it is not wrong to let yourself be bound in this way.

Line 6 *'Cockcrow rises to heaven.*
Constancy, pitfall.'

The cockerel's crowing rises to heaven; the cockerel does not, nor does his crowing cause the sun to rise. You are making noises you cannot match in reality. This enters realms of over-ambition, leaving inner truth behind: instead of trusting, you demand a response, trying to force a connection and define how things shall be. But there are limits to the changes you can create with your words. When you are overreaching yourself, persevering in your agenda will not help, and is likely to damage relationships.

Hexagram 62, *Small Exceeding*

Key Questions

Do you need to cross a line?
What small things can you do to meet the needs of the situation?
How can you take even more care?

Oracle

'Small exceeding, creating success,
Constancy bears fruit.
Allows small works, does not allow great works.
A bird in flight leaves its call,
Going higher is not fitting, coming down is fitting.
Great good fortune.'

Exceeding, or 'going past', is a transition, the moment when you step over a line. And 'Small Exceeding' means making this crossing in small ways: going beyond boundaries and structures, but paying close attention to them, always responding and adjusting, like a humble traveller crossing over great mountains.

This is a creative way to engage with the world, no matter how small you feel. You're in no position to realize great things all at once, but it is worthwhile to do the smaller things that *are* within your capacity, taking small steps with consistent purpose.

Small Exceeding is like a bird in flight: small, exposed and vulnerable as it crosses over a vast expanse of sky. It must come down and settle eventually, and even as it passes by and is gone, its call reminds you not to go against your nature and overreach yourself.

For your own unique call to be heard, you need to fly closer to the ground and pay attention to details, creating a more sensitive connection with your world. When you come down to earth in this way, scaling down your aspirations, crossing over in small ways and doing small works, then you enjoy *great* good fortune.

Image

'Above the mountain is thunder: Small Exceeding.
A noble one in actions exceeds in respect,

In loss exceeds in mourning,
In spending exceeds in economy.'

Distant thunder is heard far over the mountains. A noble one's actions rest on a firm knowledge of limits, but also go just a little beyond them - like the soft sound of the thunder, carrying beyond its origins. He will do more than is expected of him to honour a transition, paying careful attention to what is irreversible, and exceeding what might be considered sufficient and 'sensible' in his response. So he shows more respect for all involved, mourns the losses more freely – and also takes more care over expenditure, making provision for the future.

Sequence

Small Exceeding follows from Hexagram 61, Inner Truth:

'To have trust naturally means acting on it, and so Small Exceeding follows.'

When you are filled with inner conviction you are naturally moved to action. The truth you experienced inwardly becomes a message you must carry safely out into the world.

CHANGING LINES

Line 1 *'Bird in flight means a pitfall.'*
The bird feels under pressure; it reacts by taking flight, when it would do better to stay close to the ground. If you react without taking time to understand, you're liable to overreach yourself – and also to isolate yourself from supportive connections.

Line 2 *'Going past your ancestral father, meeting your ancestral mother.*
Not reaching your ruler, meeting his minister. No mistake.'
To create sustainable relationships and patterns of living, you need to concentrate modestly on the practicalities, on what is attainable. So in relationship with your ancestors, as you reach out to connect with the spiritual powers behind experience, you would go past grandfather and meet with grandmother: you bypass the origins, don't attempt to engage with reasons why, but instead go straight to *how* things take shape.

Likewise, there is nothing wrong with being unable to access or influence decision-making when you still have scope to work on the way things are done. You can engage with the 'minister', finding how best to carry out decisions or live with choices already made. This modest approach may prove more useful than seeking out original causes.

Line 3 *'Not going past, he defends himself.*
Someone following may strike him down. Pitfall.'

Instead of moving on, you dig in and defend your chosen position. Perhaps it seems as if, in staying with what you know, you are defending your vision; after all, you have no idea what you might encounter out in the wider world beyond your ramparts. So rather than completing the transition, you take your stand, and convince yourself you can make it work. But it's most unlikely that you can repel reality when it encroaches on all sides; there will surely be something you don't see that brings you down.

Line 4 *'No mistake.*
Not going past, meeting it.
Going on is dangerous, must be on guard.
Do not use ever-flowing constancy.'

Even if you don't feel wholly secure, you are where you need to be. Rather than forging on through, you can make an authentic connection here. You meet with truth – and you need to *respond* to this encounter, ensuring that you meet the demands of the situation with precision and care. To go on regardless, in just the same way as before, would be dangerous.

This is a time to take changing circumstances into account and know when to desist, rather than being doggedly true to your chosen way. And it is good to be prepared, as if with your weapons to hand, so that you can move confidently in any direction.

Line 5 *'Dense clouds without rain*
Come from our Western altars.
The prince hunts with tethered arrows,
And gets the one living in a cave.'

Offerings for rain were made at the Western altars, and now the clouds are approaching – but until the rain falls, the crops cannot grow: potential cannot be realized until conditions change. The prince is setting out to change things; he does so by shooting into a cave or pit with 'tethered arrows' – arrows attached to strings, like miniature harpoons, for retrieving game.

This means moving into a position where you can exert more influence and reach more help, and acting directly to bridge gaps and draw what you need towards you. By 'hunting' within a smaller area, you can maximize your chances of getting a result; by trying something that's *likely* to work, rather than waiting for guarantees, you can bring out whatever potential may be hidden in the situation.

Line 6 *'Not meeting at all, going past it.*
Flying bird leaves.
Pitfall, rightly called calamity and blunder.'

You fail to connect with the situation and what it requires; instead, you over-extend yourself and attempt more than is sustainable, like a flying bird that never rests. The bird leaves; the message you needed to hear is lost to you; you are out of touch with the reality and do not learn. The disaster that follows is partly because you didn't understand the situation clearly.

Hexagram 63, *Already Across*

Key Questions

What is decided?
What now?

Oracle

'Already across, creating small success.
Constancy bears fruit.
Beginnings, good fortune – endings, chaos.'

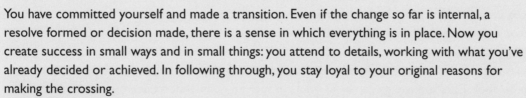

You have committed yourself and made a transition. Even if the change so far is internal, a resolve formed or decision made, there is a sense in which everything is in place. Now you create success in small ways and in small things: you attend to details, working with what you've already decided or achieved. In following through, you stay loyal to your original reasons for making the crossing.

The Zhou forded the river and overthrew the Shang dynasty. As they established their rule, they had in mind how the Shang once received the Mandate of Heaven to replace a corrupt dynasty. Now the Shang had forfeited the Mandate and were ending in chaos, while the Zhou enjoyed fortunate beginnings. Might the story repeat itself? It's easier to create new, clear-cut patterns for living than to live by them.

It's not that what you have begun here must inevitably fall apart. Only if you feel as if you've 'arrived' already and let yourself come to a halt, then you lose your path and *then* it all falls apart. Work with what you've accomplished so far, and keep your momentum: keep on beginning.

Image

'Stream dwells above fire: Already Across.
A noble one reflects on distress and prepares to defend against it.'

Water above the fire is like a pot on the boil: a productive meeting of opposites that will last just as long as you pay attention to both the fire and the water level. So a noble one has presence of mind, awareness clear as a flame within the stream of emotional experience. If you are mindful of anxieties, contemplating them with an open heart, you are well placed to anticipate and ward off trouble.

Sequence

Already Across follows from Hexagram 62, Small Exceeding:

'Going past others naturally means crossing the river, and so Already Across follows.'

Always going a little further than is expected, having the courage of your convictions in the small things – eventually this amounts to a substantial commitment, and you complete the crossing.

Pair

Already Across is paired and contrasted with Hexagram 64, Not Yet Across

'Already Across: calm and settled.'
'Not Yet Across: exhaustion of the male.'

All is decided and in place; everything is working. Yet this already implies that there is more work to be done. Feminine energy can be at home in such an open-ended, uncertain state; masculine strength, that acts to achieve and complete things, will be exhausted by it.

CHANGING LINES

Line 1 *'Your wheels dragged back, your tail soaked – no mistake.'*
You've driven your carriage through the ford, but its wheels slip back down the bank. Or you're like a fox (as in Hexagram 64) who has made it across the river, but still suffers the embarrassment of a wet tail. Your journey into the new territory is not going smoothly; you are hampered and slowed down. But this is not a sign you're going the wrong way; it's simply a natural consequence of crossing a river and entering terrain unknown to you. Things are bound to be unclear and unsettled at first. Slowing your expectations to keep pace with the circumstances gives you an opportunity to orient yourself.

Line 2 *'A wife loses her carriage screen – don't chase it.*
          On the seventh day, gain.'
As it crosses the river, a woman's carriage loses the curtain that screened her from the world. A loss leaves you exposed, insecure and lacking in optimism. However, pursuing what you've lost would take you away from your path and back into deep waters: you could easily be dragged under by anxious thoughts and lose more than just a carriage curtain. Better to focus on your destination, and have faith that what is

yours will come back to you at the right time – perhaps what you lost, perhaps something better.

Line 3 *'The high ancestor attacks the Demon Country.*
Three years go round, and he overcomes it.
Don't use small people.'

The Demon Country bordered Shang (and later Zhou) territory, undermining their peace and prosperity with constant raids. It was subdued by a Shang ruler at the cost of a long, hard campaign.

Demon Country is whatever lurks at the periphery of your life, disturbing your peace, threatening your achievements, and always returning to haunt you. If you decide to tackle this, it will take sustained effort and you will need to choose carefully which voices to listen to as you select your strategy. The small people would naturally take the easier option, and adapt to Demon Country rather than confronting it; they would let its influence creep back in, for gains made against Demon Country are easily lost. Such a responsive, accommodating attitude is of no use to you now. You need instead to think of laying the foundations for what you want to build here in years to come.

Line 4 *'The leaks are plugged with clothes of silk.*
For the whole day, on guard.'

This is more like being in a leaky old boat than safely across the river: a fragile situation, still in transition. What feels whole, sure and smooth for now must wear out in the end; better to put it to use to make running repairs and keep afloat. Until you reach firm ground and a new pattern of living, you will have to watch tirelessly for any sign of trouble.

Line 5 *'The neighbour in the East slaughters oxen.*
Not like the Western neighbour's summer offering,
Truly accepting their blessing.'

The Shang were wealthy enough to make extravagant sacrifices of any number of oxen, while their Western neighbours, the Zhou, were limited to more modest offerings. Yet it was the Zhou who had, and valued, a true bond with the spirits. You are not asked to give more than you have; great offerings are not called for here, and can be counterproductive. The offering is not an achievement or an end in itself; what matters is the sincere, lasting connection and relationship it creates. That connection can be damaged by over-complication and doing too much, but is sustained by keeping what you offer simple and true.

Line 6 *'Soaking your head. Danger.'*

After crossing the river comes the backwash; after the transition, everything stirred up by the change is not so easily left behind. When you are still immersed in and befuddled by the experience, you can easily let your self-possession slip away so that you are swept off course. There is a danger of losing your forward momentum and being pulled back into old ways. You need to remember your original objective and build actively for the future.

Hexagram 64, *Not Yet Across*

Key Questions

How to prepare for the crossing?
How will you know when it's time?

Oracle

'Not yet across, creating success.
The small fox, almost across,
Soaks its tail:
No direction bears fruit.'

Here at the very end of the Yijing, nothing is settled or complete; everything is in flux.

A wise fox will only attempt to cross when there is solid ice on the river, and then pick his way over carefully, every sense alert. If he sets out when the conditions are not right, he won't be able to complete the crossing: he'll be shamed and stranded at best, and he may be altogether sunk. For a small fox on drifting ice in midstream, there is no useful direction.

When you are not yet across, you may be hesitating on the verge of a transition, trying to tell whether it's safe to commit yourself. It's time to use the skills of a wise fox.

Image

'Fire dwells above stream: Not Yet Across.
A noble one carefully differentiates between beings, so each finds its place.'

There is fire and there is water – the right elements to cook with, but in the wrong places relative to one another. The next task is to find better places for things, so they can work together coherently.

A noble one uses the qualities of fire above and stream below: a careful, respectful awareness of the undercurrents, like the acute eyes and ears of the fox attuned to the river's flow beneath the ice. She will develop her understanding of how the different elements and processes in a complex situation fit together, and find ways for people to relate more harmoniously.

Sequence

Not Yet Across follows from Hexagram 63, Already Across:

'Things cannot be finished, and so Not Yet Across follows – and so the completion.'

While there's life, there is change, and no transition can be the end. Everything is in place and then nothing is in place; you arrive, yet you have barely begun. All that completes is the cycle itself.

CHANGING LINES

Line 1 *'Soaking your tail,*
Shame.'

The little fox sets out for the far bank, but soon discovers the river. Since he has only just started to cross, he's not stranded like the fox of the Oracle, but still hampered and shamed.

Acutely aware of the distance between where you are and where you feel you are meant to be, you start out without too much thought. Then you realize to your embarrassment that you don't know exactly how to continue, and may not be able to finish what you've started. However, there is still time to turn back or change your approach.

Line 2 *'Your wheels dragged back.*
Constancy, good fortune.'

Taking your cart down the riverbank at a headlong gallop is not necessarily a sign of courage – it may just mean anxiety is driving. It's better to slow down as you approach the water, to bring your momentum under control and give yourself a chance to see the best way to proceed. Choosing a speed you can sustain enables you to complete the crossing safely.

Line 3 *'Not yet across. Setting out to bring order: pitfall.*
Fruitful to cross the great river.'

Change is underway, and it's important not to underestimate the scale of it, and to contain your frustration at all the things that aren't working.

Before the Zhou could found a new order, they had to cross the river into Shang territory; before you can create the results you want, you need to make your decision and take a risk. Even if it's entirely reasonable to want guarantees – or at least reassurance – first, you actually need to commit yourself before things can be worked out. This is how you establish something new – not by forcing it, but by undertaking a process of change.

Line 4 *'Constancy, good fortune, regrets vanish.*
The Thunderer uses this to attack the Demon Country.
Three years go round, and there are rewards in the great city.'

The 'Demon Country' bordered Shang territory, and menaced it constantly with raids and unrest. It had been subdued in the past (see Hexagram 63, Line 3), but the 'Demons' renewed their attacks, and the 'Thunderer', a Zhou general, defeated them once again on behalf of his Shang ruler.

There is a personal Demon Country – an ever-present source of disquiet haunting the periphery of your life, always threatening to sabotage what you are building. Because this is a long-standing, recurring issue, it will naturally take a long time to deal with it now – but if you overcome your uncertainty and act decisively, *it can be done*, and you will reap the rewards. There is an opportunity here to expunge regrets and start afresh.

Line 5 *'Constancy, good fortune, no regrets.*
A noble one's radiance.
There is truth and confidence, good fortune.'

You are still not yet across, but there need be no regrets – you are working in the present for change. With a clear understanding of what change is needed, you can take the initiative with steady conviction. When your confidence in a successful transition shines like a beacon in all you do, you inspire trust and invite good fortune.

Line 6 *'Being true and confident in drinking wine.*
Not a mistake.
Soaking your head,
Being true and confident, losing your grip on that.'

You are *almost* across the river; Yi suggests you start the celebrations now. Imagine how it will feel to have completed the crossing; be truly present to this desire and vision, and have confidence in it. There's no mistake in becoming a little intoxicated with the possibilities: this is a way to liberate your essential strength from whatever fears and inhibitions have hindered your progress. It frees you to be more involved, more energetic, more spontaneous – and simply to move in your chosen direction.

However, there is a fine line between disinhibition and delusion. To 'soak your head' is to become very drunk, to lose yourself in that river you still need to cross. When you find your own truth, it's easy to get caught up in the vision and forget that it isn't yet real. You become more confident than ever in your personal grasp of the situation – just as you are altogether losing your grip on it.